MW01194358

THE MAN NO ONE BELIEVED

THE MAN
NO ONE
BELIEVED

*The Untold Story of the
Georgia Church Murders*

JOSHUA SHARPE

W. W. NORTON & COMPANY
Independent Publishers Since 1923

For information about permission to reproduce selections from this book,
write to Permissions, W. W. Norton & Company, Inc.,
500 Fifth Avenue, New York, NY 10110

For information about special discounts for bulk purchases, please contact
W. W. Norton Special Sales at specialsales@wwnorton.com or 800-233-4830

Manufacturing by Lakeside Book Company
Book design by Daniel Lagin
Production manager: Gwen Cullen

ISBN 978-1-324-02071-4

W. W. Norton & Company, Inc., 500 Fifth Avenue, New York, NY 10110

W. W. Norton & Company Ltd., 15 Carlisle Street, London W1D 3BS

To my late grandmother,

Lunette Hilliard Carpenter,

for raising me on her stories.

CONTENTS

A NOTE ON DIALOGUE

Dialogue written in italics is recalled by people who were involved in the conversations. When dialogue is in quotation marks, the words are taken directly from transcripts, recordings, or official documents or were heard and recorded by the author while reporting.

THE MAN NO ONE BELIEVED

Prologue

Off the side of a lonesome dirt road in Coastal Georgia, a group of African American residents came together to build a church. It was small and modest with a cross outside—a beacon for the weary. Rising Daughter Baptist Church rose in 1900, planted fourteen miles from the Atlantic coast near the marshes off the Little Satilla River. At Rising Daughter, members fell in love, got married, baptized children, and mourned losses. Those who'd gone on were buried in the cemetery next to the church, where the constant humidity deposited green algae on the gravestones, along with tufts of Spanish moss that fell like tinsel from the oaks. Despite the challenges they faced in the years after the Civil War, Rising Daughter's congregation of a few dozen people took comfort in the history their kin had forged there. Like many Black churches, Rising Daughter was a place of refuge against the terror of Jim Crow and a haven to organize resistance. The local NAACP held meetings there for many years, continuing into the 1980s, a time of seismic change for the community.

For generations, most people in the rural county, including members of Rising Daughter, worked in agriculture, shrimping, or at the

Gilman Paper mill. But in the 1980s, after the construction of the Kings Bay naval submarine base, Camden County began to transform. The Kings Bay base, whose name comes from the plantation that once stood there, held the government's East Coast cache of nuclear warheads. As the Navy moved in, the population boomed, the job market expanded, and Camden County, which was 66 percent white, became more diverse. The base also drew occasional disarmament and anti-Reagan protesters, but that was a trade-off worth accepting. Tourism to picturesque Cumberland Island—whose beaches were once a getaway for scions like the Carnegies and Kennedys—was flourishing, and politicians reminded their constituents that the nuclear base, even if it seemed a little menacing, was ushering in a new era of progress to South Georgia.

But for many people in countryside communities like Spring Bluff, where Rising Daughter was located, it seemed not much had changed. In 1985, you could still walk down the road in Spring Bluff and wave to the grandmothers shelling peas on their front porches and the folks working in the fields. Pulpwood crews were hauling pine trees to Gilman Paper's factories, the same as generations had before them. Off Highway 17, Rising Daughter and its cemetery remained, with concrete angels holding vigil over the graves of church members who'd been born into slavery. Politicians could claim that they were building the future, but for the Black community in Camden County, the past was always present, and a "new Georgia" had yet to arrive.

One March night in 1985, all those myths about peace and progress seemed shattered. In an unimaginable act of violence, a beloved couple was murdered, and Rising Daughter would be transformed from safe haven to crime scene. The cruel tide of history would return to Camden County, plunging Spring Bluff into seemingly endless investigation fraught with lies, missteps, and tragedy. For over forty years, the investigation has been passed like a grim baton from the hands of investigators, one after another, each searching for the truth and justice. But the full story of the murders has never been told because too much mystery remained. Now the story can be told.

THERE WERE FORTY MILES BETWEEN THE FRONT DOOR OF MY childhood home and Rising Daughter Baptist—that's nothing when you live somewhere as sprawling as South Georgia. I'm the son of two people with deep roots in the region, and both sides of my family worshipped at churches like Rising Daughter Baptist: small, roadside sanctuaries where members joyfully prayed in the same rooms that their families had for generations. Most Sundays, my immediate family went to a large, new church in Waycross, where I felt bored and out of place. But I loved to go to the small family churches and hear hymns sung in the very same pews and in the very same way my grandparents heard them. In these hallowed rooms, I felt history and the present colliding, like waves on the backs of the ancient sea turtles on Cumberland Island. Even as a kid I felt the power. I knew that family churches meant even more for my African American neighbors.

From an early age, I visited Camden County—Georgia's last stop before Florida—numerous times: the waterfront in St. Marys, the bluffs on the north end, downtown Woodbine. As a young man, I was a regular at the Woodbine Opry, a former elementary school where on Friday and Saturday nights, locals would take over the auditorium to play bluegrass and classic country. I remember the white-haired couples slow dancing to Patsy Cline's "Crazy" and other love songs from their youth. I played pedal steel guitar for the raucous crowds at Captain Stan's Smokehouse, also in Woodbine, and watched as little clouds of dirt would rise from the ground as they danced under the moonlight.

On sunset drives, I marveled at brilliant colors painting the sky above the spreading marshes.

As a journalist, I came back to Camden County to tell stories about hurricanes and rural politics—assignments I volunteered for because of my history in, and love for, South Georgia. The investigative projects I felt most drawn to were often South Georgia stories meant to hold powerful people and institutions to account. I wrote about a fourteen-year-old girl who ended up buried in her family's backyard near Savannah after state child welfare workers ignored a dire warning about abuse in the home. I exposed how the railroad that built my hometown, Waycross, poisoned the ground with carcinogenic waste for generations, and I examined if it could've sickened four local children with the same rare cancer. I covered the flaming downfall of a boisterous Camden County state representative who was run out of office after shouting the N-word and mocking people of color on Sacha Baron Cohen's TV show *Who Is America?* The stories I covered were shocking and often painful, but they felt necessary. I believe that justice depends on people knowing the truth.

IN SUMMER 2019, THE GEORGIA INNOCENCE PROJECT CONTACTED me about the double homicide at Rising Daughter Baptist Church. The murders took place in 1985, the year before I was born. I was surprised I'd never heard of the case, which was one of the most horrific crimes in modern South Georgia history. Over the phone, the nonprofit's executive director sketched out the details. One night in March 1985, a strange white man showed up at the church. He pulled out a gun and murdered a deacon named Harold Swain and his wife, Thelma Swain—a beloved couple who'd been married four decades and knew everyone in the community. The shooter escaped into the night. The crime had been major news in Georgia when I was a toddler and was even featured on the show *Unsolved Mysteries*. But then it faded into memory. When I first heard about the murders, the dynamics—a white man kills people in a historic African American church—reminded me of the 2015 horrific racist murders of nine people during Bible study at Emanuel AME Church in Charleston, South Carolina. The white gunman in Charleston was vocal about his hateful motives. I wondered whether the cases could have something in common: that same racist rot at the core of much violence in the South, and America writ large.

There were plenty of Camden County officials who said the case was settled long ago, that there was nothing left to learn. Yet, the more I learned, the more stunned I was. Decades after the murders, there remained huge questions about why and how it happened and, critically, who was involved. The Georgia Innocence Project wanted to know if I'd be interested in trying to make sense of the case, knowing that I was from Waycross. The nonprofit didn't know that my family history also made me more open to potential innocence cases. My maternal grandmother's brother Huey died in prison when I was young, and I grew up hearing about how he'd been convicted for a murder he didn't commit. I don't know if he was innocent or not, but I know the belief that he was innocent caused decades of torment for my family. As a journalist, I'd spent a great deal of time with families who'd lost loved ones to homicide, and I tried desperately to convey the contours of their pain.

I'd covered a lot of homicides by the time I heard about the murders at Rising Daughter, but what I learned about this crime and its tangled aftermath floored me: multiple confessions by different suspects, major disagreements between the detectives, and a rumor mill that was still spinning. It was unlike any murder case I'd ever heard of—and one of the most horrific and infuriating. As I dug further,

I also discovered numerous connections to players in the case. For decades, my late paternal grandmother, a dental hygienist, cleaned the teeth of the prosecutor who worked the case. Relatives of friends had heard rumors about the murders and met suspects. I had social media friends in common with more than a few of the players, though I knew none personally. One of the victims, Harold Swain, was born in the same county—Ware—as me, seven decades earlier. We both grew up exploring the Satilla River, eating the catfish it gave, and spending time in the soggy, piney woods where the Okefenokee Swamp tried to swallow up dry land. I decided to investigate the murders, hoping my history in the area would help me catch things that others didn't.

Knowing South Georgia as I do, when I wondered about the killer's motive, I naturally considered racism. Back in 1985 (and even still today), there were plenty of hardcore bigots around South Georgia, and many of them could be violent. I'd also heard stories about long-haired drug traffickers who ran wild in the backwoods, hiding bodies in the swamp. And I'd heard about the short-tempered country boys who would kill you just to vent because their dog lost a fight. It turned out that investigators had considered all kinds of men in this case—and the investigation still seemed far from finished. My efforts to investigate the various suspects led me on a mind-bending and intense journey through the back roads of several states and into many dark corners, where sources warned repeatedly that danger still lurked. They said that the wrong man had been charged, that the murderer was still at large.

One day in early 2020, my phone rang. It was one of the suspects.

"What is the point of all this?" he asked, sounding agitated by my investigation. "I hope y'all find out who actually did it. I had nothing to do with this. I want it to stay where it is—gone."

I couldn't let that happen.

PART I

WAVES

In Coastal Georgia's salt marshes, the tide pushes weakly, deceivingly. You can wade out and feel the tide glide past you, behind you. The marsh is so slow, so ill-defined and yet encompassing, that you can imagine the tide is just gone. When day ends, the sky draws your eye to kaleidoscopic sunsets. Catch the right one, and it might be the most remarkable thing you've ever seen: brilliant washes of red, yellow, and purple. You might be struck silent, letting the crickets and fiddler crabs screech and sing. That's how you forget about the tide. But the tide comes back.

1

The Man in the Vestibule

A bare yellow bulb hung over the front door of a small church of white cinderblock. The moon waned. A young man walked across the grass toward the door.

It was a Monday night in March 1985, and twelve congregants were inside, studying their Bibles. In the front row, a burly deacon flipped the pages of his worn King James version. Sixty-six-year-old Harold Swain had grown up in this room. He'd been born in nearby Ware County, but when he was just a boy, he went to live on his grandparents' farm in Camden County. Swain grew up attending Rising Daughter Baptist and had led the Sunday school program for half his life. If Spring Bluff, a predominantly Black, unincorporated community of a few hundred people, had a mayor, it probably would have been Harold Swain.

Swain built his life on hard labor. For decades, he harvested pine trees to feed area mills, employing a small crew that included church members. Now he was mostly retired, but he was a church deacon and kept himself busy. A lot of people knew him as the nice man who helped run Choo Choo BBQ, a local favorite for pulled pork, and the attached gas station. There was only one other store in Spring Bluff, Reed's, and scarcely any other businesses. Neighbors had to look out for each other. Harold Swain was known as someone who would be there when there was a problem that needed solving. He'd stop by neighbors' houses just to ask if they needed help in the yard. He was dependable, a protector.

THAT NIGHT, THE MAN CLIMBING THE STEPS TO THE FRONT entrance, with the yellow light shining off his hair, wore dark clothing and cowboy boots. He stepped inside and stood alone in the vestibule. The double doors to the sanctuary were closed. He leaned against the wall and waited.

The sanctuary was one long room with geometric stained glass windows, rows of dark wood pews, and white flowers flanking the altar. Congregants were holding a meeting of the church's mission department, which included Bible study. Swain's sixty-three-year-old wife, Thelma, was the secretary of the mission group. She sat at a table near the front, in her brown glasses and striped shirt, diligently taking notes.

Harold and Thelma Swain had been married for forty-three years. Thelma grew up not far from her husband on her family farm and had attended Rising Daughter Baptist all her life. After she married Harold, he started his logging business, and she took care of things at home. They were never far apart for too long, the type of couple that just fit. She cooked breakfast for the two of them every morning, and at 6 p.m. she had dinner ready for whoever was there, which often included her nieces and sister, who lived down the road. The Swains adopted a grandniece who became their only child, and at various times over the years, the couple had taken in two of Thelma's brothers.

Harold, who led Bible study for the mission group meeting, was the only man at the church that Monday night. Around him sat ten women—all of them homemakers and nurses—and one seven-year-old girl. The group was made up of women from different churches in the area. They were: Vanzola Williams, Marjorie Moore, Lettie Frazier, Gwendolyn Owens and her seven-year-old daughter Leslie Owens, Vandora Baker, Mattie Owens, Louise Baker, Lottie Bell Clayton, Cora Fisher, and Thelma Swain. Most of them had known one another for much of their lives, and their children had grown up together in this sanctuary.

Vanzola Williams glanced at her watch and saw it was nearing 9 p.m. Her daughter needed a ride home from work at K-Mart in Brunswick, the port city and largest town in the area. Williams was fifty-five and soft-spoken, with a slight figure and thick-rimmed brown glasses. She raised her hand and said she had to leave, then said goodbye and placed her dues payment on the table in front of Thelma Swain.

When Williams pushed open the door to the vestibule, she found a white man who appeared to be in his twenties leaning there with his arms crossed, one scuffed cowboy boot on the floor, the other up on the front door. Startled, Williams jumped back a step. *You want something?* she asked.

I wanna talk to somebody, he said.

Who you want to talk to? Williams pushed the sanctuary door open so he could see inside.

He stuck his head through the door and craned his neck. *That man there.* He pointed to Harold, seated with Bible in hand.

Williams walked down the center aisle and touched Harold on the shoulder. *Deacon Swain, there's somebody want to see you.*

Harold rose and laid the Bible down on his seat. It was turned to Ephesians, a book about a great mystery unraveled. In it, the apostle Paul writes of the revelation he'd received about the love of Christ, a boundless love that grants peace and eternal life, forever and ever. In a broken world, Harold believed in that endless love.

Harold approached the man. *You want to talk to me?*

Yes.

Harold tried to lead him outside, but the man said he wanted to talk right there in the vestibule. Vanzola Williams wasn't worried—people often stopped by the church to ask for food or gas money. Poverty was deep and gnawing all over South Georgia. Helping people was core to the church's purpose, and members didn't turn away folks in need. Vanzola Williams left the two men to speak and went on to her car.

As Thelma Swain read aloud the last meeting's minutes, she noticed everyone's attention on the vestibule door, which Harold had left cracked. *Y'all done got me nervous now*, she said to the back of the women's heads.

Thelma stopped reading at the sound of a commotion: loud thuds and shoes slapping on the floor. The women jumped up from their seats, and some ran to check on Harold. The two men were face-to-face, tangled up. The stranger had a concealed handgun. He pulled it out and raised the weapon. Harold kept fighting. The white man squeezed the trigger, cracking a shot through the air, then three more in quick succession. In an instant the women who'd been running to Harold's aid were running for their lives, dashing toward the back exit.

Thelma was the only one who kept rushing forward, shouting, *Harold is shot!* When Thelma pushed open the door to the vestibule, Harold was slumped against the shooter, struggling and trying not to fall. The man had his arms around Harold, holding him up. The moment Thelma appeared, the gunman pointed the weapon at her and pulled the trigger.

Vanzola Williams had been about to climb in the car when the sound of gunshots snapped through the dark. She raced down the side of the church, running past the cemetery where the graves of loved ones and ancestors lay—Robinsons, Fraziers, Dallases. She heard a fourth gunshot. She pulled open the back door to the church and slipped inside. She hid in the kitchen.

In the sanctuary, two women were left. Cora Fisher had fainted and fallen between pews. The other, Marjorie Moore, was frozen where she stood, unsure which way to run until she rushed out a side door, through an anteroom, into the kitchen where there was a phone—but she couldn't get it to work. Moore, the hard-charging sixty-year-old president of the mission department, ran to the pastor's study with his phone in mind. She found that nearly all the other women had beaten her there. *Nobody called the police?* she asked.

They'd tried. The phone was dead. *Oh my God,* Moore said.

The women prayed, then waited in pained silence for twenty minutes. They hoped Harold and Thelma were OK, but they had no idea if they were alive or dead because they hadn't seen if either was hit by the bullets they heard. But if the Swains weren't shot, where were they? Finally, Moore spoke up. *Somebody has got to get out of here and go get some help.*

He might still be out there, a voice said.

Moore decided to see for herself, with Lettie Frazier, sixty-two, following behind to make sure Moore was OK. They sneaked through the kitchen, out the back door, which opened to darkened woods by the graveyard. Moore walked slowly to the corner of the building and peeked around. She couldn't see anyone.

As Moore crept back inside and returned to the other women in the pastor's study, she realized that she was the only one who still had her purse. That meant Moore was the only one with car keys. *Y'all pray I get to my car,* she said, fishing them from her bag.

Moore grabbed a broom as a makeshift weapon, holding tight to the handle as she raced to her car. She threw herself into the driver's seat, started the ignition, and peeled out of the churchyard, forgetting to close her door. She drove toward the nearest store, Reed's Package, and after what felt like a lifetime but was more like one minute, she arrived and jumped out of the car.

The man's down there shooting them, she shouted at the store's owner, Gregory Reed. He swept her into his own car and sped to the church.

When they arrived, the scene was quiet. To Reed, the church, with the front doors closed, looked still as a painting, peaceful as ever. But inside, there was terror. The woman who'd fainted had come to and crawled across the floor and was hiding in the secretary's office. The others were huddled in the pastor's study, trying not to make any noise, praying, praying, praying that the gunman wouldn't come in and shoot them.

Marjorie Moore and Reed were worried the shooter was still inside, too. They drove a short way down the road to pick up one of Harold Swain's cousins who could help if there was a confrontation. The three approached the door. Reed pushed open the door to the vestibule. The gunman seemingly was gone, but he'd left hell behind. On the floor, Harold and Thelma Swain lay drenched in blood, dead. Thelma's hand touched the back of Harold's head, as if comforting him.

2

The Officer's Duty

By 9:40 p.m., when Chief Sheriff's Deputy Butch Kennedy pulled his cruiser into the churchyard, the scene glowed with intersecting beams of headlights. A dozen or more vehicles were there, with more arriving carrying loved ones of the Swains and the witnesses, as well as police from various nearby agencies. Kennedy had done a long shift that day, then worked in the yard at home, and hadn't gotten around to taking a shower when the phone rang: two people fatally shot at Rising Daughter Baptist Church. Kennedy had thrown his uniform back on and rushed there. His adrenaline was rising, as it would in any murder case, let alone a double murder in a church, when he walked toward the front steps where a few cops were gathering. Kennedy climbed the front steps, looked into the vestibule, and prayed he was in a nightmare.

Kennedy was forty, clean-shaven, five-foot-ten, and trim, and, like the vast majority of other Camden County sheriff's deputies, white. He was a Vietnam vet who didn't talk about it, and between his eyes, he bore the jagged memory of a smashed beer bottle he caught while breaking up a backwoods bar fight. Kennedy wore the standard local deputy's uniform, and in his pants pocket he carried a coin embossed with a Jesus fish that his wife, Patsy, had given him. He wasn't religious. But through the osmosis of hot Sunday mornings and his mother's lessons, Kennedy picked up on the basics. He believed his purpose was to help others.

Kennedy saw Harold and Thelma splayed on the gray tile. The air still smelled of acrid gunpowder mixed with the soft florals of the women's perfumes. There was so much blood. Kennedy reached out and touched the wall to make sure this moment was real. It was. He felt himself starting to panic. He hadn't heard it was the Swains who were killed. They were some of the nicest people he'd met since he'd moved to the county. He would see Thelma in Brunswick when she did her Friday shopping, and he often chatted with Harold in the parking lot outside Choo Choo BBQ.

Kennedy's habit was to document crime scenes, in addition to taking photos, by describing what he saw into a cassette recorder. He clutched it, and with a swampy voice, said: *shell casings, glasses, blood smeared across the floor.* He didn't say everything he was thinking. His mind was speeding away: *Who the hell did this? You don't do this and get away with it—definitely not here.*

Butch Kennedy became a deputy on April 1, 1973. He'd always assumed it was his destiny to follow in his father's footsteps. His dad was a sheriff's deputy in Telfair County, to the northwest of Camden County, and Kennedy grew up in—actually lived in an apartment under—the jail. At night, he sat and listened to the incarcerated men tell him stories and jokes through the bars. He called some of them his friends. One man who was allowed to have some tools made him a toy: a windup crane of cardboard and wood scraps. When he wasn't playing around at the jail, young Butch sometimes hit the road with his dad as he responded to calls, settled disputes, and checked on folks. The boy was shy, more of a listener than a talker, and he liked how his dad's job gave him the opportunity to get to know people. Arrests seemed rare. The job was, day to day, about helping folks. Kennedy wanted to help people like his dad did. Three decades later, he was proud to be chief deputy in Camden County.

Kennedy had worked homicides before, but his daily routine was closer to that of a traffic cop than a homicide investigator. The county had at most a couple murders a year—typically domestic violence cases, barroom fights taken too far, or gas station robberies gone wrong. The cops here almost never saw a homicide without an obvious motive. Murders were normally over on the coastal side. Spring Bluff was one of the most peaceful, low-crime corners of Camden County, a swampier version of where he grew up. The only shooting that ever happened around here was from hunters. Kennedy could barely imagine what the witnesses were feeling.

THE SHAKEN WOMEN WERE STILL GATHERED BY THEIR CARS IN the churchyard. Amid the adrenaline, Kennedy felt a jolt of something he hadn't expected propel him across the grass toward the women. It wasn't confidence. Maybe it was a speck of optimism when he needed it. He knew he was responsible for finding the gunman who broke these people's hearts. As stunned, anxious, and, yes, scared as Kennedy was, he figured there were only a few people around here who were capable of opening hell like this. All the detective needed was a witness to say something memorable about the gunman so he'd know which of the local "hellions" he needed to hunt down. Kennedy had also summoned help from state police, and a group of agents were on their way to help in the investigation.

Kennedy heard that one of the women, Vanzola Williams, had spoken with the killer. The detective found her surrounded by a humming crowd. In the spray of competing headlight beams, Kennedy couldn't see if Williams was crying, but he knew she was upset, and he tried not to make it worse.

"Everything you give us is gonna help us to get this cleared up," he said. "And I know—I know that right now is a trying time, but I—if you'll just tell me everything . . ."

"OK," Williams said, her voice gentle. "OK, I came to the front of the church to the door and there was this man standing there."

"If you could see him again, if you saw him again would you recognize him?"

"I think I would recognize him," she said, thinking a second then repeating, "I think I would recognize him."

~

THE NEWS THAT NIGHT CAME IN AGONIZED PHONE CALLS AND urgent knocks at the door. To the Swains' daughter. To their nieces and nephews. To Harold's brothers and sisters in Florida and his cousins. To Thelma's sister, brother, and cousins. To their friends and neighbors. All night, the churchyard swelled as more people arrived from all over. In the moments after the shooting stopped, the church had been eerily quiet. Now the churchyard was swelling with police, the Swains' loved ones, church members, neighbors. They walked or drove or ran to the scene. People asked each other for details and shared what they knew. A theory emerged among church members: maybe a passerby who'd been trying to beg from Harold Swain or rob him ended up shooting him. That was the best anyone could come up with. But why, everyone seemed to be asking, did Thelma get killed? It was no surprise that she'd run toward her husband in his moment of need; that was who Thelma was. But why had the murderer killed her too? Out of anger? Panic? Because the other congregants had run out the back of the sanctuary, Thelma Swain seemed to be the only person who saw the gunman fire the fatal shots. Only she could have seen the look in his eyes.

JOE GREGORY'S PHONE RANG AT HIS HOME IN BRUNSWICK. HE was an agent with the Georgia Bureau of Investigation, the agency a small-town chief sheriff's deputy called when his department needed backup. Joe Gregory immediately started driving toward Rising Daughter.

Gregory had extensive training in crime scene preservation and investigations, much more than most Camden County deputies. He carried special kits and tools and manuals. Kennedy didn't even have any evidence bags on him. He was glad to have the agent's help. Gregory and Kennedy had worked together on cases before and grown to respect each other. It was well-known that Camden County Sheriff Bill Smith had a habit of micromanaging high-profile cases. If the sheriff became overbearing, Gregory was a good partner in resistance.

Gregory was a Vietnam vet who talked about it. He had a thick, dark mustache, the broad-lensed glasses of the day, and a voice stitched up tight like cops on detective shows in the fifties. And like a blustery film noir cop, he would tell you what he thought about most things. Gregory might be wrong, very loudly. But he let you know that you could count on him.

When he pulled up to the church at 10:30 p.m., Gregory already had a sense of what he was about to see and had steeled himself for it. After much experience, he found he could control his adrenaline and focus on the work after a tragedy. The emotional processing would have to wait. He knew how to breathe through it and remember how critical it was to gather as much information as possible instead of getting bogged down in heartache. Such was the case when he began the grim task of documenting the scene in the vestibule.

He took photos and stretched measuring tape across the room. On a blank sheet of paper, he sketched the crime scene, noting the precise location of the bodies and various items. Thelma's glasses were still on her face. One pair of glasses on the floor belonged to Harold, perhaps thrown from his head as he fell. A third pair of glasses lay on the tile, inches from the bodies. The lenses were worn and oily, and the temple pieces were mismatched. No one at the church could place them. Gregory and Kennedy assumed that the killer must've dropped them during the fight with Harold or as he fled. Stuck in the hinge were two hairs that appeared dark blond or light brown. Not that hair would do much for a detective in 1985, the year DNA testing was pioneered and many years before its standard use in criminal investigations.

Looking over the scene, Kennedy and Gregory didn't know what the items meant, but they knew that the meaning could sneak up on an investigator. Even with scant evidence, Kennedy and Gregory could already make some educated guesses. Whoever did this didn't seem to plan it very well because he'd had to leave in such a hurry that he forgot to pick up his beat-up, MacGyvered glasses. The glasses seemed like another promising clue: even without DNA testing, small dents in the lenses appeared to have come from some type of welding.

Whoever did this seemed to have come with bad intentions: on the side of the church, the telephone wires had been cut.

"OK, NOW, HE WAS A WHITE, A WHITE..." KENNEDY WAS double-checking.

"A white man," Vanzola Williams said.

"And he was dressed in black?"

"In black."

"In black pants too?"

"Black pants and black shirt," Williams confirmed. "And he had long blond hair hanging down." She gestured to her shoulders.

Though Williams didn't hear what Harold and the man said after she left them talking in the vestibule, she didn't think from what she had heard that Harold Swain knew the visitor. Kennedy never asked Williams anything about a racist motive, and she didn't mention anything about it. Williams was an excellent witness, Kennedy thought. She was observant and specific about what she saw, what she didn't see, what she wasn't sure about, and what she knew for certain. Kennedy had been hoping Williams would say something about the killer that reminded him of some guy the sheriff's office had already dealt with. It was common for people who killed to start with other violent crimes and land on local police radar. But nothing about this killer sounded familiar. Kennedy worried that the shooter wasn't someone local cops knew. Interstate 95, which spanned the entire East Coast, was less than three miles from Rising Daughter.

In the days that followed, a TV news station in Jacksonville, Florida, the nearest large city, would air a segment on the murders, which included photos of the victims and a description of the suspect as a white man. The reports didn't raise the possibility of racism as a factor. *The Brunswick News* gave no indication of the victims' race or that Rising Daughter was an African American church. But local Black residents and leaders had their own understanding: Thomas M. Baker, president of the Camden County chapter of the Southern Christian Leadership Conference, told *The Southeast Georgian* that his organization suspected the attack could've been racially motivated and called the shooting a "heinous act of violence." Baker knew the local history.

He knew that Camden County didn't have a public high school for Black students until a lawsuit forced construction in 1952. In 1984, just months before the murders, Baker and other African American residents sued Camden County to change local election policy that disenfranchised Black voters. Baker knew all too well about the hate that had been behind the county's racist policies.

"We are urging that the sheriff's department move quickly on this matter so that the person or persons responsible for these cold-blooded murders will be apprehended," Baker said.

FOR CAMDEN COUNTY'S BLACK COMMUNITY, THIS DOUBLE MUR-der was part of a terrible, familiar history. Since its settlement, the bloody histories of slavery and dispossession have defined the region and define it still. For the congregants of Rising Daughter, a church founded by people whose families had been enslaved for generations, segregation and racial terror weren't distant, abstract histories. They were living memory. Violence was etched all over the Camden County landscape—one local deer hunting spot, "The Gallows," was named for the site of an 1840 lynching—and with the double homicide at Rising Daughter, it truly seemed that nowhere was safe.

Yet white community members liked to imagine that racism was history. Former plantations could be wedding venues, and Confeder-ate leaders could be lauded for their bravery in "the War of Northern Aggression." Their racism could be envisioned, like so many things, as a spectrum. There were white people in Camden County who loved their Black neighbors, there were white people who weren't much interested in race, and there were white supremacists. There were white folks who could work side by side with a Black person for decades, say racist things around them without a second thought, and then cry at their funeral. In this culture, almost all white people possessed enormous blind spots about the troubles of their Black neighbors. This was particularly true in Kennedy's generation.

Kennedy had grown up during segregation in the hometown of Georgia's arch segregationist governor, Eugene Talmadge. In comparison, Camden County in 1985 seemed like a big improvement. Segregation had ended, the Voting Rights Act passed, and it seemed like the promise of equal opportunities could be realized. As chief deputy, Kennedy helped the sheriff's office hire more African American deputies than ever, and he didn't see his duty to his Black neighbors as any different than to his white ones. A person was a person, he would say, and simply by virtue of being a person, everyone mattered.

But people like Kennedy simply couldn't feel racism's presence on the same visceral level as their Black neighbors. A conspiracy of violence and willful ignorance had resulted in a prevailing feeling that race—and especially racism—wasn't proper to bring up in public. So, many Black people didn't voice their concerns around white people. And because they didn't ask, a lot of white Georgians could convince themselves that racism wasn't a serious problem anymore.

Kennedy, who worked all over Camden County, knew that Georgia was still home to plenty of extremely racist people. But when racist sentiments led to violence, it was at most a fistfight—not a double murder. He hadn't asked the church witnesses if the killer said anything to indicate a racist motive, and none of them mentioned it. Kennedy discussed the possibility of racism as a motive with Joe Gregory, and in the coming days, they sought out intelligence about local hate groups, but they didn't learn much. The detectives didn't think racism made much sense as a motive. As naive as he would later realize it was, Kennedy had only ever heard folks—Black and white—say nice things about Harold, and he struggled to imagine the hate that would drive someone to kill such a kind man.

EARLY 1980S: INTERSTATE 95, EXIT 26. SPRING BLUFF, GEORGIA.

Harold Swain chopped the wood, loaded it into the battered smoker, lit the fire, and stoked the coals. Sweet smoke rose into the sky. How many people smelled that delicious combustion emitting from the grill at Choo Choo BBQ, passing by on I-95? Tens of thousands? Millions? As families passed through on their way to Florida's theme parks— EPCOT's gigantic golf ball was brand new, just two hundred miles from Spring Bluff—Swain labored over the smoker and greeted those who stopped to try the legendary barbeque sauce. Locals were loyal customers too. And not just because of limited options. "We've been stopping here since weeks before forever began," a customer once said. "We'll keep stopping after forever is over."

This was a lonely stretch of I-95, where that smoke could appear as an oasis amid the pine trees and palm fronds. Choo Choo BBQ was attached to Rawls Store, a convenience store the shape of a ranch-style house, where high school kids pumped the gas and Swain helped everyone with everything. Here was Swain handing out a rib plate to a construction worker. Here he was carrying a woman's bags to her car. Here was Swain counting out change behind the register while the clerk took a break. Here he was with a smile asking how he could help you.

3

The Killer's Face

When Kennedy rose the morning after the murders, at his home in the heavily wooded White Oak community, he was angry. *Harold and Thelma Swain.* He was having trouble absorbing it. *What did they ever do to anyone?*

Kennedy dressed in his usual deputy's uniform—minus the hat, as always. It was one of those with the circular brim and the two dimples in the crown—too conspicuous for the detective. Kennedy put on his belt and holstered his 9mm, the only accessory he carried besides a pair of handcuffs. No mace, flashlight, or radio. He had to gird himself for a day of interviewing terribly traumatized people. At the same time, he couldn't wait to start the day because he believed the interviews could lead to a breakthrough.

The Camden County Sheriff's Office had always been a smaller agency, but that never seemed to matter because there wasn't much serious crime. Today, though, Kennedy felt ill-equipped. He climbed in his cruiser, an unmarked light blue Chevrolet Chevelle, and set off for Spring Bluff. When he pulled up, the morning was warm, without rain. But he'd be sweating soon. On the marsh-side land not far from the Okefenokee Swamp, humidity was always with you.

Kennedy started by interviewing a church witness. Cora Fisher was fifty-two, a homemaker and mother of five. She lived down a sandy dirt road near Rising Daughter. Fisher had been so traumatized by the shooting that she sought medical attention at the Brunswick hospital, but the doctors couldn't find the right medicine to calm her down. She was thinking about going back to try again, and when Kennedy saw her, he understood why. The woman couldn't stop shaking as she recalled watching Thelma run to try to help Harold.

"When she pushed that door open, I could see the pistol," she told Kennedy, trembling. "He shot her just like that."

Kennedy's face soured. "Good Lord!"

Fisher turned to Kennedy and twisted her face into a look of pure menace. "He looked at me just like I'm lookin' at you . . . And then he kinda smiled."

Who could do such a thing and then smile—in a church?

Fisher told Kennedy that she didn't know what happened next, because right after that look, she fainted. When she came to, she found the sanctuary empty and quiet. Propelled by terror, she'd crawled across the carpet, clutching her purse, imagining the gunman following right behind her. She kept glancing back to be sure he wasn't there. She hid in the secretary's office until church members came by to check for occupants. When they opened the door, Fisher fainted again.

Kennedy hated that someone did this to her, to all of the women at the church that night. As she spoke, Fisher would fall silent, caught by her thrumming nerves. "I don't know why he didn't shoot me," Fisher said, tears in her eyes. "I was lookin' dead at him and he was lookin' dead at me."

"I know that's a bad feeling," said the deputy.

"Just to see the, just to see the—" she couldn't finish the thought.

"I know it's a bad feeling," Kennedy said into the silence. "I can't feel the way that you do, I know." As much as he empathized, pausing to give Fisher a moment, he knew he had to ask a question. He hated feeling like he was injuring people. But he had to ask now, before the memories faded forever.

"Would you recognize him if you saw him again?"

"Yes," she said. "I'll never forget."

Could she help make a sketch? She would try.

One more question: "Do you know anybody that would have a reason at all to hurt Harold or Thelma?"

"I thought about that all night," she said. "I don't know if he made enemies with somebody . . ." She trailed off.

"Harold didn't make enemies, I don't think," said Kennedy.

Fisher agreed, still shaking.

After talking with Fisher, Kennedy drove up and down Highway 17, passing Rising Daughter each time he headed from one witness's house to the next.

GREGORY LOOKED LIKE HE'D BEEN THROUGH A STORM, WAS still in it, when he blew past his wife, Pat, in their home that Tuesday morning, just hours after the Monday night murders. Life had been going well for the high school sweethearts after a period of adjustment in South Georgia. Gregory moved to the area to work as a state trooper. But he'd got into a few too many tiffs with the local lawmen. Gregory had the urge to speak up when he saw a rule not followed—a form not filled out, a torn-up ticket for a friend of the powerful—and had frayed some relationships with the state troopers. The Georgia Bureau of Investigation, where his job gave him much more authority and responsibility, proved a better fit.

When he left the house, Gregory headed just down the road to the Brunswick hospital, a recently expanded tan structure with palmetto trees in the parking lot. He went to the morgue with the state's chief medical examiner, who flew around the state on a private plane to perform autopsies in high-profile cases. Gregory, taking notes to relay to Kennedy, already knew that they could be working on the most significant case of their careers. They had never fathomed something so depraved happening here: the murder of a beloved couple and, most gallingly, the fact of a brutal crime taking place in a church.

The doctor removed Thelma Swain's body first. Dried blood trailed from her mouth, down her cheeks, and into her ears, which were still studded with gold earrings. He removed the paper bags Gregory had placed on her hands to preserve any evidence. Thelma's palms were streaked with blood. Her right hand was still clasped around a blue-and-white Bic pen, medium point.

The bullet had torn through Thelma's upper right chest, near her collarbone. The doctor followed its trajectory to her spinal canal, where he found a loose copper-jacketed projectile. The medical examiner removed it and looked it over. It was in relatively good shape. A .25 caliber, the doctor guessed, the kind of ammunition typically used in a small, lightweight handgun. The gun would have been easy to conceal for the element of surprise.

Under the harsh lights and amid the hum of machines, the doctor examined Harold Swain's body. He wore a dark blue windbreaker, with that space-age matte-shimmer finish that seemed ubiquitous in the 1980s, and a blue work shirt with bullet holes in it. While Thelma's body was laced with blood, Harold was drenched in it. He'd been shot three times in the chest and once in the top of the head, sending the bullet into his upper back. The doctor removed four more .25 caliber bullets. Harold's windbreaker was dusted with gunpowder. The doctor sent the bullets and the Swains' clothing to the GBI crime lab for analysis.

As he stood there, looking at the Swains' bodies and contemplating what kind of person could do this, Gregory was angry and confused. He prayed that Kennedy was finding something.

KENNEDY'S CHEVELLE BUMPED FROM THE PAVED HIGHWAY TO another dirt road. He stopped at the Swains' modest home, cinderblock like so many in the area, where numerous people had been coming and going. The house hummed with uncertainty, shock, agony. Thelma's kitchen was full of people, knowing that the smell of her cooking would never fill the house again. They looked at Harold's chair and knew he would never again sit there, washed in the glow of the evening news or studying his Bible. Everyone was most concerned for the Swains' daughter, a grandniece they'd adopted when she was about three. LaFane, now twenty years old, had lived with them for seventeen years but would soon return to the sometimes complicated home situation she'd left. Inside that white cinderblock house in Spring Bluff, worlds were burning.

Kennedy stopped to pay his respects, but he also needed to interview any witnesses who were there. He found Gwen Owens among the crowd of mourners, and she seemed to have seen as much as Vanzola Williams.

Owens was thirty-four, a nurse at the same Brunswick hospital where the Swains' autopsies had just been performed. Her seven-year-old daughter, Leslie, had been in the church on the night of the murders, too. It was the first time that Owens and Leslie had attended a Mission Department meeting at Rising Daughter; the department featured members from a few area churches, including the one where Owens worshipped. Kennedy was accompanied by GBI Agent Lee

Sweat, who led the interview with the mother and daughter while Kennedy listened.

"Last night when you were at the church and the door opened and the man looked in, did you look at him?"

"Yes," Leslie volunteered, "he had on some kind of black glasses and a red mustache and red hair."

When asked to elaborate, the girl demurred. "Ask Mama."

No one else mentioned red hair or a red mustache. Maybe "red" was the closest color Leslie knew to the color she saw in the man's hair. Or maybe she only thought she saw him. The detectives focused on her mother's account.

Gwen Owens, shaken as she was, tried to replay what happened in her mind before she told Sweat and Kennedy. She said she'd been seated on the red velvet pew next to Cora Fisher when Vanzola Williams got up to leave.

"Trying to think now, be careful," she said.

Owens remembered Williams, after meeting the strange man in the vestibule, tapping Harold Swain on the shoulder.

"When I looked back," Owens told the officers, "there was the fellow sticking his head around the door. . . . And he had hair almost the color of yours, it looked like." She gestured to Agent Sweat's hair, a darker brown than Kennedy's light hazel. "It was long and it was split down the middle. He had on black rim glasses. He was either wearing navy blue or black shirt and pants."

Owens said she'd had a good view of the vestibule from her seat, and she had seen Harold struggling with the man. Owens could see the man's face for a moment before he turned with his back to the sanctuary. Owens recalled the white man as clean-shaven, though she wasn't sure if he'd had a mustache. But she clearly remembered glasses.

Vanzola Williams and Cora Fisher hadn't mentioned this, but Owens was certain. "I was leaning over peeping," she said.

Owens wasn't sure how many shots she heard in total. At least two.

Leslie thought she knew. "My daddy say . . ." Her mother stopped her. "You don't go by hearsay," Owens corrected.

Kennedy was trying to reassemble the crime in his mind. One witness had said she thought she'd heard someone come in a while before Vanzola Williams saw him in the vestibule. Was the assailant waiting to rob the collection plate, which held Mission Department dues payments from the members? It was about enough money for a cheap record player or a weekend of beer money, and it went untouched. Botched robberies turned into murders all the time, Kennedy knew, particularly when somebody fought back. He'd talked to Harold enough and seen the way he carried himself. Harold would fight back.

"And how loud did they say they were gonna take up the dues," Kennedy asked.

"Did somebody say, 'Get your money out'?" asked Sweat.

"Somehow or another, yeah," Owens said, "the money was mentioned."

ON CHANNEL 4 *EYEWITNESS NEWS*, OUT OF JACKSONVILLE, FLOR-ida, the segment on the murders opened with a man perched on top of a picnic table with other mourners, his expression pained. They shook their heads in disbelief. One man ashed a cigarette and grimaced.

"The town is still in a state of shock," said the female voice-over. "Almost everyone in Spring Bluff knew the Swains. They can't believe this has happened."

In the next shot, Vanzola Williams sat with a reporter on a couch in a wood-paneled room at the Swains' house. Williams was composed, well put together in a white cardigan. "Before I could get the car door open, I heard the shots. Four shots." Williams said Harold and Thelma were bighearted people who looked out for their neighbors. "I just don't see any reason for this to happen."

In another frame, it was Marjorie Moore on the couch, looking like she hadn't slept in days. Moore was the brave witness who grabbed a broom and went for help. She was a powerful woman. And she looked shattered. "I don't know, I'm kind of numb. Then sometimes I get shaky," she said, starting to turn her head side to side. Her eyes dug into the carpet. Her voice filled with pain and slowed down. "I just don't want to believe that it really happened. It's just one of those things you see happen, but you still yet don't want to believe."

A tight shot of the steeple at night pulled back to reveal the news anchor standing in front of Rising Daughter. "Church members say it won't be easy to come back here," she said. "But they'll continue to hold their mission meetings to pray that the suspect is caught. Robyn Sieron. Channel Four Eyewitness News. Spring Bluff, Georgia."

DOWN AT THE SHERIFF'S OFFICE IN WOODBINE, TWO DAYS LATER, Kennedy and other detectives helped witnesses use Identi-Kits—a box of paper noses, lips, eyes, mustaches—to arrange an outline of the killer's face on a table. "OK," Kennedy said to Marjorie Moore, "there's six billion faces in this little box right here. You're gonna build one that resembles or is similar to the person that you saw in there. Anything that you aren't satisfied with, we can change it. There's no problem at all, 'cause we want to get as close to the person that you saw."

Before fleeing for help, Moore had briefly seen the killer's face through the cracked door. Her description essentially fit with what the others had said, but she agreed with Gwen Owens that his hair was black while two others thought it was blond. Moore said she knew Owens had seen glasses, but she didn't see any on the man. "Because he lost 'em in the fight," Kennedy speculated.

Moore arranged the face, as close as she could, on the table. So did the other three women who said they'd glimpsed it. In a few days, a sketch artist would drive up from Jacksonville and try to compile their paper faces into a single picture. In the meantime, investigators would have to keep searching and examining what they already had.

"We feel like there's a possibility that robbery was the motive," Sheriff Bill Smith told *The Brunswick News*, "though I'm not at liberty to disclose the evidence at this time." The sheriff said he "definitely" thought the killer was the one who sliced the church's phone lines. Smith said the killer may have stalked the victims ahead of the robbery and then aborted the plan after the shooting, leaving $300 in Harold's wallet and the women's purses, along with cash in the collection plate. In the article, police described the car believed to have been driven by the killer as "a medium brown 1965–70 model Dodge Dart or Plymouth Duster."

The media loved to publish descriptions and sketches from unsolved crimes. It helped people feel like they could be a part of the solution. Police sketches had been around for hundreds of years and would remain commonplace. This sometimes-decisive piece of evidence relies on something ephemeral: an eyewitness's ability to remember a face and describe it in language that can be replicated. The process is further complicated by the way trauma has been shown to impact memory. The biggest problem might be this: Resemblance is in the eye of the beholder. And when you're searching for a criminal, you may see what, or who, you want to see.

But in the days before DNA testing and ubiquitous security cameras, investigators worked with the tools and methods they were given, unaware of how horrifically unreliable some of their training would prove to be. It was and always would be extremely hard to solve homicides. Killers take steps to hide evidence, and witnesses may be too afraid or too traumatized to provide reliable identifications of suspects. Kennedy and Gregory were doing what they were trained to do and what they believed worked, but like every other detective of the day, they were stumbling through the dark—even sometimes when they thought they were close to the truth.

A FEW DAYS AFTER THE FOUR WOMEN DESCRIBED THE KILLER, the sketch artist studied the Identi-Kit faces assembled from their memories. Three of them depicted a young man with collar-length straight hair. Cora Fisher's sketch, Kennedy was later puzzled to notice, looked a lot like Alfred E. Neuman, the big-eared character grinning on the cover of *Mad Magazine*. Fisher's story about the killer smiling at her before she fainted was compelling. But the more Kennedy thought of it, the more he wondered if Fisher saw the killer's face at all. There would've been a door between them, according to Gregory's map of the scene. He believed that Fisher was genuine in saying she saw his face, but she might be mistaken in all the drama.

The artist appeared to ignore Fisher's sketch when combining them for the composite. He told Kennedy the women were generally happy with the composite, except for Gwen Owens. She didn't think the composite looked like the killer. Kennedy didn't like the sound of this, but protocol said they needed to release a sketch.

So they released the sketch: a slender white man, probably in his twenties, with wavy, shoulder-length dirty blond or light brown hair and a prominent forehead and chin. Within hours, the composite slithered out of fax machines at police departments across the country. It ran in newspapers and on TV, and wanted posters hung in gas stations for miles. At the bottom of the page was a request to contact investigators. And more than a few people would study the drawing and see someone they knew.

4

A Cross for Everyone

Cynthia Clayton, the Swains' twenty-five-year-old niece, was still in shock on the morning of the funeral. She had spent five days and nights in anguish. Just hours before the murders, Clayton had gotten off work at a nearby Head Start program and driven to Spring Bluff. She lived a short walk, one taken often, from the Swains' home. Driving down Dover Bluff Road at around 5:30 p.m., she saw Harold standing in his yard, doing something near the pump faucet for the water well. She honked and waved, and her uncle waved back. About four hours later, she heard the news: Harold and Thelma were gone—shot inside the church. It was unfathomable.

She raced to pick up her brother, and they went to the church. Cynthia wanted to see the scene, to see evidence of this unbelievable act herself. She walked toward the front door, but someone stopped her before she could see her aunt and uncle's bodies. Like everyone else, for the funeral at Rising Daughter Baptist, Clayton would have to walk over the spot where they'd lain.

On the afternoon of the service, a band of rainstorms blanketed the South. Clayton arrived to find the churchyard filled with mourners, sidestepping puddles in their dress shoes. The storm filtered through the tree canopy, splashing onto the graves in the cemetery. Even in this weather, people had driven from all over Georgia and Florida. The sanctuary, which could hold maybe 150 people, was packed, each pew full and some attendees standing against the walls. The Swains' remains lay in matching cream-colored caskets with silver hardware. Thunder cracked in the distance.

Cynthia Clayton looked around and wondered why no one had thought to move the service to a larger church. Maybe they had and thought better of it. This was the Swains' church, and there was a righteous defiance in holding the celebration of their lives here. The killer hadn't scared congregants away. But before the service began, Clayton decided she couldn't do it. The loss—the *theft*—was too much to handle. She knew her aunt and uncle would understand, so she left, walking back out into the rain.

Soon, the crowd in the church rose to sing.

Must Jesus bear the cross alone
And all the world go free?
There's the cross for everyone
And the cross for me

The mournful swing of the melody engulfed the sanctuary and encouraged people to slowly sway. They didn't have to bear this jagged cross alone, not as they filled each pew of the countryside church where the wound was opened.

Though the funeral was for the couple, family and friends planning the service had been careful to honor Harold and Thelma as individuals. The funeral home made two programs. But Harold's and Thelma's lives were so intertwined that their obituaries differed only slightly:

The late Mr. Harold Swain was born July 4, 1918, in Ware County, Georgia. He was the son of the late Mr. and Mrs. Andrew Swain. He moved to Camden County, Georgia at a very early age. He was married to the late Thelma Lang Swain on July 28, 1941. He became a Christian at a very early age at the Rising Daughters Baptist Church, where he served as a deacon, and was Superintendent of Sunday School for over thirty (30) years. He departed this life March 11, 1985.

The late Thelma Lang Swain was born December 25, 1921, in Camden County, Georgia. She was the daughter of the late Mr. and Mrs. Jimmie Lang. She became a Christian at a very early age at the Rising Daughters Baptist Church where she served in Choir Number One and as Secretary of the Mission Department of the church for over thirty (30) years. She departed this life on March 11, 1985.

So many people wanted to speak that each was limited to three minutes. One after another, they rose to memorialize the Swains, emphasizing their service to others. Harold grew up working with his grandparents. He helped Spring Bluff by attending county government meetings and speaking up for the neighborhood's needs. He was a baseball fan—he saw Jackie Robinson's barrier-breaking 1955 World Series debut in person—who successfully lobbied the county to bring a park with a diamond to Spring Bluff. Harold was the area representative in the Camden County NAACP and ran Spring Bluff's volunteer fire department, which was little more than a truck parked at the Swains' house and promises from neighbors to help if a fire broke out.

Thelma grew up working on her mother and stepfather's farm. She taught her nieces to cook and made Clayton a quilt to remind her of home when she went off to college. Thelma went to her little sister's softball games and made her laugh constantly; she was less the joke-telling type than she was the type who could find humor in most anything. When her brother suffered from intense flashbacks to traumas he endured in World War II, Thelma brought him into their home so she could look after him and drive him to treatment. After his death, when Thelma's other brother with failing health came from New York for the funeral, Thelma talked him into moving in with her and Harold.

Harold and Thelma were buried beneath the oak trees, mossed over from the coastal humidity. Umbrellas blocked the rain as mourners gathered to see pallbearers carry the Swains to their resting place. A spot had been chosen near the back of the cemetery in the church's side yard. They faced the sanctuary. There was no message inscribed on their joint headstone. Just two hands, held together, praying.

IN THE DAYS AFTER THE FUNERAL, NUMEROUS CALLS CAME IN about the sketch. Kennedy and Gregory, along with other assisting GBI agents and deputies, worked their desk phones and drove across South Georgia to check out the dozens of men whom tipsters claimed could be good suspects. One was a man who frequented a store at the Kings Bay naval base over on the coast and reportedly acted strangely. One was a man who walked into a Georgia State Patrol office to have his license renewed and looked off to the license examiner. Another man frequented a gun shop and spewed racist vitriol.

The detectives had to check everyone's alibi. Kennedy and Gregory found people's bosses and mothers and wives and drinking buddies. In cases where they couldn't provide an alibi, the detectives would call the man's eye doctor. They wanted to see if the men's prescriptions could match the repaired, beaten-up pair of glasses found near the Swains' bodies. None did.

As more days passed, Kennedy's frustration got to him. He'd been sure—*certain*—that the case would be solved quickly and that he'd be the one to solve it. But in the first two weeks, the sheriff's office had received three hundred calls and investigated an expansive list of suspects, and yet the murderer seemed to be getting away with it. Kennedy had no doubt that he was failing the people of Spring Bluff. But he kept this feeling to himself and worked.

In late March, a press conference was called by a diverse coalition of officials: Sheriff Bill Smith, pastors of area African American churches, businessmen, the presidents of the Camden and Glynn County NAACP chapters, and officials from Woodbine. They were raising a $10,000 reward for information leading to the arrest and conviction of whoever killed the Swains. Governor Joe Frank Harris's office had agreed to put in another $2,000.

"We've received calls about this despicable case, as despicable as any," said Reverend E. C. Tillman, of Brunswick's Shiloh Baptist Church, "but the good citizens of this area, good Christian people have decided to do something in a positive vein." A white Kingsland businessman helped organize the fund and residents were encouraged to donate at any bank in Camden County. "There has been tremendous concern that such a coldblooded murder could've taken place here," he said, "but for it to have been done in a church is a desecration of the Lord's house."

A reporter asked the organizers whether race could be the motive.

The reverend, who was Black, acknowledged that some feared that the crime was racially motivated, while striking a cautious note: "I think some of the church people are fearful, but until this man is apprehended, this can't be looked at from a standpoint of race to race."

Sheriff Bill Smith already had an opinion: race wasn't involved. He borrowed the microphone from the pastor. "For those who knew Harold and Thelma Swain, they were well thought of in the community. They had no enemies in the community. Race is not the issue—crime and robbery are the issue."

Others, including Ben Fleming, a relative of Harold's who served with him as a deacon at Rising Daughter, questioned robbery as a motive. "Her pocketbook was there . . . and his wallet. It seems like he would have taken one of them." The sheriff had an answer for that: the man had been spooked by what happened and aborted the robbery. Drugs, however, might've been involved if the man was desperate for money to score, Sheriff Smith said. Then he said, "I think he will probably strike again. This is the type that goes around preying on unsuspecting people."

A CLEAR, MOONLIT MIDDLE OF THE NIGHT IN THE LATE 1980S. Woodbine, Georgia.

Two deputies stopped a drunk driver on I-95 and found paydirt in the trunk: $52,000 in suspected drug money. The passenger was also drunk, and the officers announced that both men were under arrest. Before being handcuffed, the passenger pulled out a Skoal chewing tobacco tin from his pocket and slung it toward the woods. It sailed, misting white powder. Call that an I-95 Hail Mary. After the deputies finished up and saw the men to jail, they took a break to catch their breath.

They met on a roadside near a bridge over the Satilla River, which reflected the light of a half-moon. Earlier, when others weren't looking, one of the deputies had slipped his hand in the bag in the trunk of the Cutlass before anyone had a chance to count. Now the deputies counted out their haul. Each man ended up with about $5,000. Working busy I-95 could be demanding, but lately, the assignment had its perks.

5

Changing and Staying the Same

Camden County was always a place of beauty and bounty—of soaring seagulls and egrets and five twisted rivers gliding into the Atlantic. If you were just passing through, you might think Camden County was a forgotten corner of heaven. But if you stayed there long enough, you'd find rot at the roots. If you read the papers, between the lines, you could see two key forces behind the local good old boy network. The first was Gilman Paper, a titan whose influence was waning. The other was the sheriff's office, whose power was ascendant like a king tide.

The Camden County Sheriff's Office was notorious and becoming more so since Bill Smith took office. Smith was a handsome charmer with thick, gray hair that belied his age—he was just in his thirties. He'd already been an FBI agent, an engineer at the paper mill, and a county commissioner, a seat he left to run for sheriff in 1984. He branded himself "Camden County's Man for the 80s" and won partly by courting the Black vote, appearing in campaign ads shaking hands with a Black community leader. Sworn in just two months before the Swains' murders, Smith picked up a reputation for lavish spending, protecting friends who broke the law, and hosting wild parties at his ranch—dubbed the Ponderosa after the family property on TV's *Bonanza*. He denied every allegation of impropriety.

Like many sheriffs in Georgia, Smith was part of a dynasty. His dad had been Sheriff Willie Smith, a Southern gentleman–type and a gifted winner of hearts who could also be cruel. Elected in 1942, he grew the agency from a two-man operation to a band of twelve deputies by the 1970s, though he still didn't employ a single Black officer. Civil rights leaders had accused his deputies of accosting and murdering Black people, in one case an African American man who was suffering a mental episode. One Black newspaper called it a lynching. In the mid-1970s, a Camden County NAACP officer who'd been mentored by Harold Swain convinced Sheriff Willie Smith to hire two African American deputies, part-time. Like his father did before him, Bill Smith stayed in power through the 1980s by making friends with the leaders of the most powerful business, Gilman Paper Company.

Opened in 1941, Gilman Paper employed thousands—most of the city of St. Marys and many county residents—at its paper mill and bag factory. It was dangerous work, but it was one of few opportunities after agriculture work tapered off. Workers put in long hours in outrageous heat, pushing logs into woodchippers, but there weren't many other options. Even those who didn't work for the mill toiled for its success in some other way. The company's accounts kept St. Marys's only real estate business, bank, and insurance company afloat. Gilman installed its mouthpieces on the St. Marys City Council and the Camden County Board of Commissioners. Gilman was everywhere, its belching chimneys depositing layers of ash on locals' homes and cars.

But the company's omnipresence brought backlash from environmentalists, labor organizers, and numerous other critics. Crusading author and researcher Ralph Nader had participated in multiple exposés on Gilman's outrageous power, once in the early 1970s calling it a "grim monument" to the American "company town tradition." Later, a *60 Minutes* crew headed by broadcasting legend Mike Wallace came to town to lay bare the punishing behemoth that was Gilman Paper.

In the 1980s, Gilman's influence was waning after the nuclear submarine base moved in. The county was transforming rapidly, which was one of the reasons Sheriff Bill Smith wanted to position himself as "Camden's Man for the 80s."

And in many ways, Bill Smith was a welcome departure from his father. He hired more Black deputies than his dad ever had, and he had friends in local civil rights organizations, including Harold Swain. Bill Smith had known Swain all his life. He made him a bondsman, which meant that Swain could, usually just with his word, have someone released from the Camden County jail. But it was the new sheriff's approach to drug smuggling that was truly revolutionary. Drug trafficking was a notorious tradition in South Georgia. A lot of sheriffs were in on it or bribed to ignore it, but Smith invented a new way to make his county's pushers work for him.

Camden County's waterways had long attracted smugglers, who used shrimp boats to move huge loads of cocaine and marijuana. But when buildup around the naval base made the routes too conspicuous, smugglers turned to I-95, the favored route for hauling drugs between Miami and New York, which took them through Camden County on the way. Smugglers would head toward the Port of Miami to stash drugs and cash in their cars, usually modest sedans to blend in with the Disney World tourists, then follow the interstate all the way north. Cocaine was a booming business, enough that busts seemed to happen on I-95 every day. The interstate, which earned the name "Cocaine Lane," required more resources and training for officers. If they suspected smuggling, deputies had to videotape themselves tearing apart vehicles looking for contraband and cash. When they seized either, deputies had to spend hours filling out paperwork and going to court. Cocaine Lane was a bad look for South Georgia and a logistical nightmare for its police.

In 1984, with drug busts soaring and growing concerns about crack, President Ronald Reagan signed the Comprehensive Crime Control Act, which included harsher penalties for people convicted of drug offenses and established a new seized asset program. With the passage of the new act, local police could share the proceeds of seizures with federal authorities. Sheriff Smith saw an opportunity. With the seized asset program, police could take the huge amounts of money they seized from smugglers and spend it. The money was supposed to be for law enforcement purposes, but the oversight was lax enough that most any definition of "law enforcement purposes" would do.

Suddenly Cocaine Lane wasn't a liability; it was a potential gold mine. Sheriff Smith decided to exploit the seized cash for his community's benefit—and for his own. His deputies would seize millions of dollars. You could see him and his deputies in the paper, photographed in front of tables full of dope and cash. He spread drug money like confetti: he threw community barbecues, gave to churches, bought people lunch. The money paid for college textbooks and residents' light bills. Smith's constituents remembered his generosity at the polls. But some of that money would come back to haunt him.

6

The Smuggler

With the extensive press coverage and attention on the case, Gregory and Kennedy faced a galling problem: too many suspects. In South Georgia in the 1980s, men who looked like the sketch of the killer—a young white guy with shoulder-length hair—were everywhere. This was the white country boy look of the day, in a land of country boys. You could've brought in entire Southern rock bands for questioning. You probably could've knocked on a random white grandma's door, asked to see a photo album, and within minutes been looking at somebody who arguably resembled the sketch. This damned reality was setting in.

Two months into the case, the detectives had investigated one hundred leads and still had no idea who the killer was. People in Spring Bluff were anxious. As much as they wanted the killer's name, they wanted to know his mind. What brought him to Rising Daughter to do this? Was it racism? A botched robbery? Was it something no one had imagined yet?

"I still wonder why somebody would stop by a church just to rob somebody, though," one man told *The Southeast Georgian*. You'd get more money if you held up a nearby convenience store.

The seeming randomness of the act was what haunted most people. "People here didn't used to even lock their doors," one resident said. "Now they're afraid not to. Some of them even wonder if the kid might not return. I don't know any reason why he would. But who knows anything about this case?"

Kennedy felt responsible for the fear running through Spring Bluff. Gregory was more open than Kennedy about his feelings, which seemed to release the pressure, and his faith kept him grounded. Gregory would've told you he was no stronger than Kennedy, but the truth is, it all dug into Kennedy deeper. He felt devastated that they—that *he*—hadn't solved the case, that he hadn't helped bring peace to the families in three long months. Gregory started leading the two of them in prayer—in the office or in the car driving to and from interviews. It felt fitting while investigating a double murder in a church. Kennedy didn't believe prayer worked, but growing up inside a jail with a devout mother, he learned that praying is what you can do when you're desperate. So he prayed. One day, he took a trip back to Rising Daughter, pacing around wondering what he was missing. He was thinking about the Swains, how good they were, how much the family must be hurting knowing the killer was still out there. Kennedy broke down and sobbed.

SUDDENLY, ONE DAY THAT JULY, FOUR MONTHS AFTER THE MURders, Kennedy thought his prayers might've been answered. The news came, amazingly, in a phone call from the Telfair County Sheriff's Office, the agency Kennedy had grown up in. They told him that a man in their jail was telling a story about the church murders.

Kennedy and Gregory arrived at the jail, which had been reno-

vated since Kennedy had lived there and was run by Sheriff Ronnie
Walker, the son of the sheriff Kennedy's dad had worked for. Butch
Kennedy and Ronnie played together as kids. They'd drifted apart:
Kennedy was a respected chief deputy, Walker a sheriff used to dodg-
ing accusations of coziness with cannabis growers, like his father had
with moonshiners.

It was surreal for Kennedy to be called back home during the
investigation. Walker welcomed Kennedy and Gregory to the jail so
they could hear the story for themselves. A few days earlier, a state
trooper pulled over three out-of-towners who had a machine gun—a
real machine gun—in the trunk. After the traffic stop, the trio faced
gun charges. One of them, a blond twenty-four-year-old Floridian
named Jeffrey Kittrell started talking about something one of his
codefendants had said a while back.

In his Panhandle drawl, Kittrell said he and the other men were
involved with a smuggling gang. Some called the loose collective of
traffickers they belonged to "the Dixie Mafia." They were a violent lot
who ran chicken and dog fights in the woods. At the time, the trafficking scene in South Georgia was largely organized around families who
did business together and traded favors or otherwise feuded. Kittrell
was still getting to know everyone in Georgia. But he knew Donnie
Barrentine pretty well. Barrentine, a codefendant in the machine gun
matter, had been Kittrell's way into the gang.

This branch of the Dixie Mafia operated out of Brantley County,
a rural area near Camden County known for little except its Confederate cemetery. The group had its home base there, a small house with
bullet holes in the ceiling from various spats or parties. Apart from the
gun play, the gang's leader and Donnie Barrentine's cousin, Greg Barrentine, lived the life of a family man there with his wife and young
kids. He employed kin and cohorts to traffic drugs into the country

from the Caribbean by boat and plane. Donnie would fly along with the cargo. Once, the story goes, he'd made the pilot land in Jamaica just so he could get a hamburger. He'd been cocky, but also an enforcer, to hear Kittrell tell it.

One night around April 1, about three weeks after the murders in Spring Bluff, Donnie Barrentine showed up at Kittrell's place drunk and talkative during a house party, Kittrell said. Kittrell and some others had been watching *Scarface* when Barrentine pulled out a 9mm handgun and started waving it around, claiming to be God.

God can give and God can take away.

Barrentine said he'd taken something. The lives of two Black people in a church.

That makes me God.

Allegedly, Barrentine said he'd gone to the church with a "cold-blooded" friend who killed the couple while he waited outside. The cold-blooded man called the "preacher" to the door and shot him, then shot his wife, Kittrell told the rapt detectives. Harold Swain was often wrongly assumed to have been Rising Daughter's pastor rather than a deacon.

Kittrell thought Barrentine said the church was in Jacksonville, Florida, the closest major city and about forty miles from Spring Bluff. That's close enough, the detectives thought, that someone who wasn't familiar with the area might call it Jacksonville.

What was the motive? Kittrell didn't know. He didn't know of any connection between Barrentine or the other drug traffickers and the Swains or Rising Daughter Baptist Church.

Kittrell also told the detectives about another murder, a pending one. When the state trooper pulled Kittrell's crew over with the machine gun, they'd been on their way to Middle Georgia. A gang leader had dispatched them there to kill a drug trafficker called Wildman. Kittrell didn't know Wildman's legal name. But this was the detail that struck the detectives: Kittrell said the gang leader had told them to kill Wildman, raid his cocaine stash, and make sure to cut the phone lines. The detectives immediately thought of the severed phone lines at Rising Daughter. It seemed like, finally, they were on their way to something.

LATER THAT DAY, THE DETECTIVES MET WITH DONNIE BARRENtine in an interview room.

"What we wanted to do," said the always understated Kennedy, "is just touch base with you and see if you could give us any information."

"Well, I didn't kill nobody, man."

Barrentine was twenty-seven, brash, and gregarious, from a landlocked town in the Florida Panhandle. He had a short mustache, shoulder-length light brown hair, and looked like he'd had a broken nose that didn't heal right. The moment Kennedy and Gregory saw him, each thought he looked just like the sketch. The hair, the light eyes, the thin face. Other people looked like it, yes, but this man *really* looked like it.

"We're not saying that you did it," Kennedy assured him. "But we've got a job to do and that's what we're here for."

Before they could get anywhere questioning him, Barrentine asked for an attorney. Kennedy said that was fine, they'd come back another time. But did Barrentine mind helping Kennedy fill in his suspect file? This involved asking for his height, weight, eye color, and the like. Barrentine didn't mind. Kennedy spied a cheap-looking tattoo on his arm.

"Is that a cross or a sword?" Kennedy asked.

"I never figured it out." Barrentine said a friend had done it while he was passed out drunk.

"Like to done a pretty good job," Kennedy said. Kennedy kept glancing at Barrentine, thinking of the sketch.

"Son-of-a-bitch was drunk, too. Passing me beer for beer. Hell, he was drunker than me."

Kennedy kept asking questions and Barrentine kept rambling, like he hadn't had a good conversation in a while. They chatted about cars and food. Kennedy said he'd been craving sweets lately; Barrentine said he ate like a horse and couldn't gain weight. They talked about guns, which brand and style was better, which was worse. Barrentine hated a .41 Magnum. Too damn heavy. He'd been offended recently when some detectives from Florida asked if he'd shot someone down there, because of the gun they thought he used. Barrentine said only a fool would use a .41 Magnum. Kennedy couldn't believe this guy's audacity.

Barrentine asked if Kennedy had heard about that other shooting.

"No, I don't know anything about that," Kennedy said. "Only one I'm concerned with is one that happened in March down in our county."

"Wait a minute," Barrentine said. "When in March?"

"March the 11th. A Monday night."

Barrentine said he would've worked his job on an assembly line in the Panhandle that day. The detectives thought he could've clocked out and made it to the church in time, though they would need to test that theory. Timing aside, they didn't have the motive they needed. Why would a drug smuggler from 250 miles away want to kill Harold Swain, or anyone at Rising Daughter? The detectives wanted to shower this man with questions. Because Barrentine had asked for an attorney, they couldn't. Kennedy asked if Barrentine minded having his picture taken. He didn't. Kennedy snapped the shot, and they left Barrentine to the Telfair County deputies.

The detectives then drove to the courthouse in Barrentine's North Florida hometown to interview Sue Wilkes, another witness to Barrentine's alleged statements at the house party hosted by Jeff Kittrell.

She was being held in the county jail on unrelated charges. "Donnie was real drunk," Wilkes said. "He usually was. . . . He had this 9mm and he was waving it around. He got to talking about being God. He said something about, 'God giveth and God taketh away and with this I'm God, because I can take it all away.' Then he got to talking about killing a Black preacher and his wife in a church. He said that the preacher was shot first and then when the preacher's wife ran through the door, she was shot, too."

The detectives now had two witnesses and would soon have a third. They'd had heard enough to believe that Barrentine had indeed said those things. But was he telling the truth? Each of the witnesses had brushed Barrentine's comment off as bragging. He was always saying he'd shot someone.

But one detail from Sue Wilkes made the detectives want to take Barrentine seriously: "He said something about being worried, because another lady saw him and fainted."

SEPT. 14, 1958. NIGHTTIME. OUTSIDE THE ST. MARYS CITY JAIL. ST. Marys, Georgia.

One night when he was nine years old, a boy heard scary news. A Black man was shot dead by a white St. Marys police officer, and his body was on the ground by the jail. The patrolman had pulled over the young man and his wife, then gotten into it with the husband. The little boy saw people running toward the jail as the night grew darker. He decided to sneak after them.

A crowd had gathered, an outraged group of Black residents who grew even more upset when they learned the name of the victim. Ernest Hunter, twenty-two, of St. Marys, was a local baseball star, a small-town hero, including to the boy. He searched for a spot in the crowd where he could see through, pushing through the bodies to see something he knew he didn't want to see. The police, evidently due to an investigation by the coroner's office, hadn't removed Hunter's body from the ground.

He'd never seen a dead body before. Here was the first: a Black man he idolized, laid out with blood on his clothes. But seven-year-old Artie Jones Jr., who would later be encouraged by Harold Swain to become the county's first Black elected official, focused on Ernest Hunter's feet. One foot was bare. On the other was one of his cleats, light brown clay from the field still stuck to the bottom.

7

The Relative

Within days of meeting Donnie Barrentine, Kennedy and Gregory pointed the car toward Telfair County again, watched the overgrown Bahia grass sway out the window again, prayed again. Jeff Kittrell had more to say. He'd told local deputies that he and Barrentine had been speaking through the cell bars and that Barrentine had revealed new information. The detectives huddled with Kittrell in the magistrate judge's chambers at the jail.

"OK, what did Donnie Barrentine say in the cell?"

"Talking about the Black Mafia," said Kittrell.

The Black Mafia was a drug-running gang headed by Wildman, the guy who they'd been on their way to kill when they were arrested. Wildman's name, Kittrell now knew, was Leon Avery. Avery was a flamboyant figure who, unlike others in the Black Mafia, was white.

Just weeks before they'd been dispatched to kill him, Barrentine's gang had been friendly with Avery and the Black Mafia. As pervasive as racism was across the South, there was a saying that in illicit business, the color that mattered most was green. To hear Barrentine talk, money was the source of the feud that left the Swains dead. Barrentine allegedly told Kittrell that the point of the shooting at Rising Daughter was to send a message to a man named Ed Brown, who was related to the Swains. Brown owed a lot of money to the Black Mafia, and he was hiding out. They decided to employ Barrentine and his cold-blooded friend to send a message to Brown through his father-in-law, Harold.

"Hit the preacher in retaliation," said Kittrell.

The detectives felt an odd mix of skepticism and fire. The story seemed convoluted. Kittrell, this shaggy-haired, rambling young man was the source. And who was Ed Brown? Kittrell called him the Swains' son-in-law. The Swains had no son-in-law. Then Kennedy remembered someone: the Swains' adopted daughter. She had a stepfather named Lawrence Edward Brown who lived in a tiny town near Savannah.

OF ALL OF GILMAN PAPER'S SCANDALS, ONE OF THE BIGGEST involved Lawrence Brown. One day in 1972, as alleged by Brown, executives approached Brown with an idea. They told him that they'd had enough of a plant worker who'd been railing against Gilman Paper in the press over its environmental record. They needed him gone. Brown said the executives, who would deny his story, offered him $1,500 to kill the man. Lawrence Brown agreed, though he would maintain that his plan was to take the money and leave town. After telling the mill bosses that he'd kill the man, he warned the would-be victim about the plan. But before Brown could flee the county, he talked to the FBI.

Brown's statement prompted an investigation. This was a perilous spot for him. He was going against Gilman Paper, whose leadership was stacked with some of the most powerful people in the county. After a conversation with two of the other most powerful local men— Sheriff Willie Smith and District Attorney Glenn Thomas—Brown changed his story. He said the paper mill bosses never asked him to kill anyone. But later he changed his story one last time, saying he only wavered because he'd been intimidated by Gilman cronies. He claimed they spirited him away to a hotel in Florida, where a man with a gun told Brown that he'd "blow my brains out" unless he testified that he'd been paid to fabricate the murder plot.

A few weeks later, Brown was driving his pickup truck when bullets shattered the windows. Brown wasn't hit, but he was taken to Gilman Hospital to be checked out. His lawyers wouldn't even let the police see him because they didn't know who could be trusted. But the FBI soon put him into witness protection and shuffled him between hotels across South Georgia until he demanded to be released.

Brown testified against the mill executives in a federal trial. The bosses were convicted of trying to cover up a murder plot but never served time because their convictions were overturned on a procedural issue. After years of fighting Gilman's monied lawyers, the government declined to try the executives again, and Lawrence Brown moved on—and up.

He started smuggling drugs, and, according to Kennedy and Gregory's sources, ended up with connections to Donnie Barrentine's crew.

WHEN THE DETECTIVES CONTACTED THE FBI, THEY WERE amazed to learn that Kittrell's story seemed to be checking out. Not only had Brown been a drug trafficker after the hitman ordeal, but he was also in federal custody at that very moment. A month after the Swains' murders, he'd been arrested in Miami when authorities caught him in possession of a storage container with 1,500 pounds of Jamaican-grown marijuana hidden behind a false wall.

Kennedy and Gregory went to see Brown in federal custody in Savannah. Brown had barely let them sit down before he said he recognized Kennedy from the night of the murders. Brown had driven to Spring Bluff and said he'd seen Kennedy in the churchyard, talking to a witness.

You wouldn't even talk to me, Brown said.

Kennedy apologized. *I don't remember you.*

Well, said Brown, *I ain't got nothin' to say to you.*

What had Brown wanted to talk to Kennedy about that night? He refused to say, and the interview ended there.

～

THE DETECTIVES CHECKED INTO DONNIE BARRENTINE'S ALIBI. His timecard showed he'd clocked out of the factory at 3:29 p.m. Gregory and Kennedy drove the 240 miles from the factory to Rising Daughter to see whether Barrentine could have arrived there by the time of the shootings. They used the best route they could find, using highways for some stretches, backroads for others. It might be tight to make it by 8:45 or so—that is, if the factory weren't in Marianna, Florida, on central time, an hour behind Georgia. The detectives pulled up to Rising Daughter with time to spare. Barrentine's alibi became even weaker when they learned that he hadn't shown up for work the day after the murders.

When the detectives assembled a lineup, Vanzola Williams picked out Barrentine, but she didn't seem sure if he was the killer. She mostly noticed his dark cowboy boots, which looked like the ones she remembered on the killer, and like the ones favored by area drug traffickers. Barrentine's shaky alibi and the detail about the boots might've played well in front of a jury. Still, Williams wasn't identifying Barrentine as the killer.

Kennedy didn't feel like he and Gregory had enough to be sure either. He wanted some sort of confession or slip by Barrentine that would make it clear. But Barrentine wasn't slipping. At least not when talking with Kennedy and Gregory. The best they could get out of him was when he once admitted that he in fact had told the party while drunkenly waving a 9mm that he'd killed a Black couple. Then he smirked and said he was lying.

IN AN EFFORT TO GET SOMETHING DEFINITIVE, KENNEDY CALLED Dixie Glenn Foster, an expert in what he termed the "kinesic interview technique," which sounded like some kind of psychic magic but was considered by some police a promising interrogation technique at the time. Foster agreed to come to Camden County and, as Foster would say, try to "become" Donnie Barrentine, to enter his mind and start looking under the couch cushions. Kennedy and Gregory waited outside a room at the sheriff's office in Woodbine while the veteran interrogator met with their suspect.

When Foster emerged, he confirmed the detectives' suspicions. *That's your man.* Barrentine had allegedly incriminated himself terribly. Foster said he'd write up a report from the interrogation and send it to the district attorney. In the meantime, Barrentine continued to deny any knowledge of the murders with the local investigators. He agreed to sit for a polygraph, or "lie detector," test. He failed it.

There was no reliable technology to determine if a person was telling the truth, and there never would be. A polygraph may detect nervousness, an understandable emotion to feel while under interrogation by police. But detectives often *believed* that these machines worked. For Kennedy and Gregory, the test was confirmation of Barrentine's guilt—and so was his response to learning he'd failed the polygraph.

Gangly in ill-fitting jail clothes, Barrentine turned to Gregory before he was led back to his cell.

Do y'all have the death penalty in Georgia?
Yes.
Well, I guess I'm gonna fry for what I did.

ON AUGUST 17, 1985, FIVE MONTHS AND SIX DAYS AFTER HAROLD
and Thelma Swain were murdered in the church vestibule, Kennedy sat
down and drew up an arrest warrant for two counts of murder. Donnie Cleveland Barrentine, Kennedy wrote, did "unlawfully and with
malice aforethought" take the lives of the Swains by shooting them with
a .25 caliber weapon. The warrant didn't mention a motive. No state
requires authorities to give a motive for murder—even at trial. Prosecutors must only prove that the person committed the crime beyond a reasonable doubt, though cases are more successful when a motive is offered.

According to Kennedy and Gregory's working theory of the
motive, Barrentine drove to the church to either attack or confront
Harold Swain to send a message to Lawrence Brown, who owed gang
members money or was expected to testify against fellow smugglers.
The detectives believed that Harold Swain fought back, and Barrentine pulled out a gun and shot him, then Thelma Swain.

Once the warrant was filed, the next step was to speak with the
district attorney for approval to proceed. Gregory approached District
Attorney Glenn Thomas for approval to proceed, even though Gregory was suspicious of his rulings in the past. Once, Gregory said, after
months of investigating the Brunswick mayor and his wife over city
credit card misuse, Thomas suddenly halted the proceedings without
explanation. The Brunswick mayor and his wife faced no indictment.
Powerful people, connected people, didn't get in serious trouble no
matter what they did. One grand jury investigation concluded that DA
Thomas was part of "the good old boy system that is so deeply embed-
ded in the County."

But Barrentine had no ties to the local good old boys, as far as Gregory knew. He expected Thomas to sign off on the warrants quickly. When they met in his office, Thomas listened to the story about Barrentine's boasts at a party about killing a Black couple. Thomas asked about the witnesses. What type of folks were they?

Gregory explained the charges some of them had faced, while also explaining that their stories aligned. Thomas shut him down.

I'm not putting druggies and prostitutes on my stand.

Well, said Gregory, *this bunch doesn't run with doctors and lawyers.*

Gregory tried to make the case that people who'd faced similar charges had been witnesses in previous cases. The detectives could've asked a judge to sign an arrest warrant, but it wouldn't do much good if the DA wouldn't prosecute. It truly was extraordinary to see the DA decline to file charges on the biggest unsolved murder case in his county, but Thomas wouldn't budge. He refused to prosecute Barrentine without new evidence—from better sources. Gregory couldn't believe what he was hearing. It was one of the most confounding moments of his career.

TWO MONTHS LATER, IN OCTOBER, A CLOSER RELATIVE OF HAR-old Swain's stopped by the sheriff's office to alert Kennedy and Gregory to something that had been on his mind. Nolan Frazier told the investigators that he had spoken with Harold Swain about Lawrence Brown not long before the murders. When Harold had taken his daughter, LaFane, to visit her mom, Brown tried to borrow $2,500 from him. Harold didn't catch what Brown needed the money for and said he couldn't help, which upset Brown.

After the funeral, Frazier said, there was a meeting of all the family members to discuss the Swains' estate. Lawrence Brown was there. Brown brought up the subject of a joint life insurance policy of $100,000, saying that his stepdaughter LaFane was the beneficiary, and he would see to it that she got what she was owed. Others explained to Brown that they'd never heard of such a policy, but he didn't seem to believe them. Frazier also said that after the murders, Brown took all of Harold's guns out of the house—about four rifles and two pistols. What he did with them was unknown.

8

"I'm the Mother Fucker"

By the end of 1985, the detectives still hadn't convinced DA Glenn Thomas of their Donnie Barrentine–Lawrence Brown theory. They kept track of Barrentine, who went to federal prison on weapon charges from the machine gun affair. They were waiting for him to run off his mouth to the wrong person again or for new evidence to shake loose. In March 1986, Kennedy and Gregory were still seething over the DA's resistance when they heard a story about a new man.

Erik Sparre, twenty-seven, had split with his wife, Emily Head, and to hear her and the family tell it, he hadn't taken it well. Allegedly, Sparre had been firing a gun through the woods near the Head family home and hollering. Sparre had also been calling nonstop, menacing Emily and the rest of the family. After one of those calls, Emily Head's father drove to the sheriff's office and told Kennedy the family had a tape at the house that he needed to hear. Kennedy and Sheriff Smith met with the Head family and listened to the tape: "I'm the mother fucker that killed the two n———s in that church," a man on the recording said, "and I'm going to kill you and the whole damn family if I have to do it in church."

The family said the voice was Sparre's. Kennedy was floored. But a sad fact made Kennedy doubt that Sparre was telling the truth: He'd heard of more than a few men telling their wives they'd killed people to threaten them. Still, this tape—a recorded, plain admission in the county's most urgent case—was something to take seriously. Kennedy knew Sparre as one of the local "hellions" and had arrested him at least twice over allegations of violence, once against Emily Head, though she later declined to press charges.

Kennedy and Sheriff Smith spoke with Emily, who had dirty blond hair, dark eyes, and a kind spirit that man after man would take advantage of. Head recalled Sparre leaving home one morning wearing dark clothing. The next morning, he returned wearing a white shirt. She said this was during the week of the murders. She left him a week later, after months of gathering strength, and soon divorced him. Kennedy knew the killer had worn dark clothes with a white shirt underneath, a shirt that lost a couple of buttons in the struggle with Harold Swain. Sparre hated Black people, said Head, who didn't approve of her ex's views and regretted getting involved with him. There are moments when an investigator's heart starts to beat faster, when the darkness they fumble through starts to flicker to light. Emily was flipping the switch.

What did Sparre do for work? She said he'd worked as a welder and as a mechanic at a trucking service. GBI scientists had found transmission fluid on the glasses from the crime scene. The report also said that the lenses were pitted, as if worn while welding. Kennedy asked if Sparre ever wore glasses. Not always, she said, but yes, he needed them. She said he'd lost a pair around the time of the murders and replaced them with a peculiar pair: one cobbled together from three old pairs of glasses from his father. Those sounded like the unexplained glasses left by the bodies. It almost seemed too good to be true.

So far, the detectives had kept information about the glasses close to the vest, as with other details that they had decided to keep out of the press to avoid letting the killer know everything they knew. But now Kennedy and Smith brought out the glasses from the scene and two unrelated pairs. They laid them in front of Emily Head. They asked if any of the glasses looked like Sparre's.

Head picked the pair found near the bodies. "Erik has a pair that looks just like these."

SPARRE WAS THE SON OF A VIRULENTLY RACIST KOREAN WAR veteran turned insurance salesman. Erik's grandfather emigrated from Denmark to Iowa, then to Brunswick, Georgia. Erik's father, Fred, was drawn to his Danish heritage and obsessed with Vikings and Norse mythology. Fred was in the Sons of Confederate Veterans, though he was once nearly kicked out of a branch meeting because members thought he was a racist extremist. He instilled his love of Confederate lore, Norse mythology, and white supremacist ideas in his son. Both men would mock Erik's mother, Gladys, for going to church by saluting and, referring to a Norse god, saying, "Heil Odin." In her divorce filings, Emily Head described Erik as a dangerous man who once held a handgun to her head and pulled the trigger. She recalled how a puff of air lifted her hair when the gun jammed.

Kennedy didn't know Erik Sparre's family, but he remembered when Sparre was accused of pulling a rifle on a person of color at Choo Choo BBQ, where Harold worked. The other time Kennedy had arrested Sparre was also outside Choo Choo BBQ, on the warrant for allegedly beating Head.

Whether Sparre killed the Swains or not, the tape was proof he threatened Head's family. Under a warrant for making terroristic threats, Kennedy arrested Sparre. But under interrogation, Sparre claimed to know nothing about the murders. He insisted he didn't kill the Swains and didn't know who did. He told them he'd been at work that night. After two days and more failed questioning attempts, Sparre was granted bond and released from jail on the threat charge.

The detectives decided to search his house. They knew he had handguns, but Kennedy wanted to see if Sparre owned a .25 caliber gun like the killer had used. In his warrant application, Kennedy mentioned that Sparre cut his hair after the murders. His hair had been down to his shoulders, Head said. His hair was brown and could've fit some of the witness descriptions. Gregory took the sketch and added darker hair, as well as the mustache Sparre wore. Kennedy presented the modified sketch, juxtaposed with Sparre's new booking photo, to the magistrate judge. Knowing Sparre had many firearms in the house, Kennedy asked the judge to approve a no-knock warrant, allowing police to enter the dwelling without first announcing themselves. The judge approved.

AT 4:30 P.M. ON MARCH 10, 1986, KENNEDY AND GREGORY ASSEM-bled near Sparre's house with the local chief assistant DA and police officers. It was a brick ranch style in a lush-green working-class neighborhood. It was one day before the first anniversary of the Swains' murders, and the case was already fading from public view. But if detectives found something incriminating at Sparre's house, all that could change.

The detectives barged in. After a heart-pounding few moments, Sparre appeared—unarmed and passive. The officers searched drawers and gun cabinets for the murder weapon, Sparre's bedroom for bloody clothes. They found nothing.

Sparre was supposed to have been working at a Winn-Dixie grocery store on the night of the murders. A few days after the raid, as Gregory would detail in reports, the agent dialed a number for Sparre's boss and spoke to Donald A. Mobley, who had been Sparre's supervisor. Mobley said he'd have to check with corporate in Jacksonville, where time cards were archived, to see whether Sparre had been working on the day of the murders. He'd be in touch.

A week later, Mobley called Gregory with the verdict: Sparre clocked in at 3:06 p.m. on the day of the murders and clocked out the next morning at 6:41 a.m. A long shift, but it wasn't unheard of. Mobley said he'd talked with employees who worked that night. "They also confirmed that Sparre was in the store on that evening," Mobley said.

Gregory had doubted that Sparre was the killer from the beginning. He'd seen men try to scare their wives with lies like this. Sparre struck him as that type. Kennedy agreed. Although Sparre was said to be hateful, they still doubted that racism was involved in the murders. They remained persuaded by the drug-trafficking theory and the fact that Sparre had no known connection to Barrentine. The detectives dropped Sparre as a suspect.

LATE 1980S. SPRING BLUFF, GEORGIA.

Lettie Frazier knew that somewhere, perhaps somewhere far or even very close, the killer was still out there. She was sixty-three when the sound of gunshots filled the sanctuary of her church. Harold Swain was her cousin. Thelma was a dear friend. That they were gone was hard enough. To have witnessed some strange white man kill them was the kind of thing a person doesn't get over, only through. Like everyone else, she prayed. Like everyone else, she tried not to think about it. Like everyone else, she couldn't help but think about it.

Lettie's son, Joe Frazier, got to know Harold Swain in the 1950s. As a boy, Joe was blown away by Harold, a young business owner. His logging company did well enough that he could buy a 1953 Ford Model A, a curvy, shining thing that could growl like a monster. Harold was among the first Black men in the area to buy a brand-new vehicle. Joe wanted to be like Swain when he grew up. Harold hired him for his logging crew as a teenager. When Joe bought his first car, he had to show the boss. Ever since the murders, he visited with his old mentor in the cemetery at Rising Daughter Baptist.

9

Unsolved Mystery

Cue the music: the staccato nightmare-inducing theme. The graphic sunburst dissolved to reveal the name of the show: *Unsolved Mysteries*.

On November 2, 1988, just days before George H. W. Bush would win the presidency in a landslide, a segment called "Slain Swain" broadcast into millions of homes across the United States. It opened with a montage of everyday life in Spring Bluff. Here's some kids riding bikes. There's a man in a rocking chair on a porch. Here is the choir leading congregants in a mournful hymn at Rising Daughter Baptist Church.

Hard cut: Dim lighting in the church at night, slow camera pans. A woman playing Vanzola Williams enters the vestibule to find a young white man standing alone. The actor playing the killer wears a cheap blond wig. The lighting is dramatic and eerie—hazy as if the camera's lens had been smeared with Vaseline.

"May I help you?" Williams's character asks.

"Yeah," the man in the vestibule says, "I wanna talk to somebody." His accent is more San Andres Valley than South Georgia, with the bravado used by so many tough guys in made-for-TV movies. "Somebody in there." He points toward an actor playing Harold Swain.

Harold and Thelma's murder plays out on the small screen: Harold struggling with the gunman as shots crack, Thelma racing to the vestibule, the handgun aiming straight for her chest when he fires one last bullet. Then the frame dissolves to show two bloodied, motionless bodies in the vestibule—actors trying hard to breathe quietly and be still. Police lights flash through the opened front door. An over-the-shoulder shot shows Kennedy and Gregory portraying themselves, examining the scene and speaking. Their words are drowned out by the soundtrack—a mix of creeping, hazy synthesizers that gives goosebumps.

Later, Gregory appears and mentions the glasses at the crime scene, how he thought the killer must've dropped them. Gregory looks at ease on camera. "The first gut reaction I had was a transient," Gregory says in a voice-over, "because the glasses appeared to belong to a person who did not have enough money to maintain glasses or to buy glasses when they needed them." The camera closes in on a pair of glasses cradled in the host's bare hands. "These are the glasses found that night," the show's velvet-voiced host Robert Stack says.

Watching the episode live from his living room, Gregory couldn't believe his eyes. He picked up the phone and dialed Kennedy. *Those are the glasses. How did they get the glasses?*

The detectives were shocked. One of their most critical pieces of evidence had been taken without their knowledge, transported across the country to reach a showrunner in Los Angeles, and was now beaming into millions of homes across America. The sheriff must've OK'd it, but that didn't make them feel any better.

It had been three and a half years since the murders, and Sheriff Smith figured that an episode on *Unsolved Mysteries* couldn't hurt.

He'd come around to the detective's theory about the murders: it wasn't a robbery attempt—it was more like a hit. He was tired of waiting for an arrest. Sure, it was unorthodox, and the title "Slain Swain" was in bad taste, but Sheriff Smith was hopeful about *Unsolved Mysteries*. The show was a runaway success and claimed that it solved four cases, including three murders. Maybe they'd receive some tips, maybe some about Donnie Barrentine.

Barrentine's mugshot and name splashed across the screen—this was the moment that Kennedy and Gregory hoped would prompt someone who knew something to say something. An actor who looked nothing like Barrentine reenacted the machine gun incident, his drunken claims that he killed a Black couple in a church, and finally, his failed polygraph test. In a voice-over, Vanzola Williams recalled picking Barrentine out of a lineup: "His complexion was a little bit lighter, but he had the same boots that I saw that night. The boots was what I recognized, but I wasn't really, really sure." She added that she hadn't been focused on the man's face that night and that the lineup had been months after she'd very briefly seen the killer, who was a perfect stranger.

As the episode closed, the host wondered aloud if the detectives would ever figure it out.

Before the segment ended, the phones were ringing at the *Unsolved Mysteries* tip line in California. The show had been watched in 13.6 million homes. More people saw the Swain segment than watched *Dynasty*, *Night Court*, and *MacGyver* that week.

Shows like *Unsolved Mysteries* and *America's Most Wanted* were bringing the public into police work more than ever, tantalizing audiences with the possibility that they could help solve a crime. Before, people interested in the case might get a sketch and a phone number to call. Now, true crime shows provided audiences with much more inside information than police typically allowed and invited viewers to help make sense of it. Detectives craved tips, and a mass audience was a way to get them.

True crime shows also represented a new process for victims of crimes to endure: to see actors reenact the most horrific moments of their lives and to know that millions of people were watching. The Swains' loved ones were galled to see *Unsolved Mysteries* use a photo of one of Harold Swain's sisters, calling her Thelma Swain. Despite the obvious errors, Cynthia Clayton, the Swains' niece, hoped the show did some good. She had been losing patience with the detectives. Unlike in some cold homicide cases, Clayton did not think her aunt and uncle's investigation was stalled because the victims were African American. But she did think that the detectives were in over their heads and weren't devoting enough resources to the case. She was struck by something Gregory said in *Unsolved Mysteries*: "They say your first hunch is usually your best. Everything that night pointed to a transient attempting to pull a robbery." Clayton thought she heard resignation in his voice. It sounded to her like Gregory was tossing his hands in the air, saying the case might never be solved.

But Gregory didn't think the killer was a passerby at all. He thought it was Donnie Barrentine. Clayton had no way to know how Gregory—or Kennedy—felt. After the first months, they no longer gave regular updates. They didn't let Cynthia Clayton or many others see how this case haunted them, though they had no intention of throwing up their hands.

TIPS CAME INTO THE *UNSOLVED MYSTERIES* CALL CENTER FROM Kansas, Florida, New York, North Carolina, Missouri, Virginia, and California, to name a few. One person thought it was a man who often robbed Black churches in Florida. One man thought he'd just seen the killer in a Jacksonville drunk tank. Another thought he saw the killer that same day, at a Texaco truck stop in Fort Worth, Texas. Someone thought it was a man who'd killed two Black joggers in Salt Lake City.

Then there were calls that sounded more logical, if not entirely helpful. A caller pointed to Harold Swain's position as a member on the local jury commission. Maybe, the caller thought, someone could have been in trouble and blamed Swain as a member of the commission. The caller, however, didn't have a suspect or case in mind.

There were two tips about one man, which was cause enough to perk up any detective's ears. Dennis Perry, twenty-six, a long-haired country guy, grew up in his grandparents' home in Spring Bluff, close to the Swains. Perry had moved to an Atlanta suburb four months before the murders. But Perry resembled the sketch—a lot.

When the composite had hit the papers, a coworker told Perry he had a twin. A relative said the same. No one took it seriously because he lived hundreds of miles from Spring Bluff, and it was hard to imagine Perry doing anything violent. The caller thought that Perry had a dark side, saying that Perry wanted to kill Harold Swain because Swain had found a field of marijuana that was somehow tied to Perry. "Dennis Perry fits the composite drawing," said the caller. "Harold Swain owned land. Dennis Perry dealed [sic] drugs to Harold's nephews. Harold found out about these dealings."

Kennedy saw the tipster's identity and realized it must've been the same person who'd given the first tip about Perry, which was anonymous and contained the same allegations. The tipster, Brian "Corky" Rozier, forty-two, was a well-known raconteur who lived near the Swains. After the first tip, Kennedy and Gregory had investigated and found that Perry had no car, didn't wear glasses, and hadn't done the type of work—welding or fixing cars—they suspected the killer had.

He also had an alibi. He'd been at work outside Atlanta finishing up late enough that even if Perry had found a car, he couldn't have made it to the church. Also, there was no evidence that Harold Swain had found any marijuana on anyone's property. Just to be safe, the detectives showed Vanzola Williams a photo spread of men including Perry. She didn't recognize anyone.

The detectives decided Perry wasn't a viable suspect. Kennedy knew Rozier, and he wouldn't trust his word for much of anything.

The calls about Barrentine were more exciting: "Check in Lakeland, Florida for Peggy Barrentine, her son fits the description of the killer. The motive is the preacher had a son who was supposed to testify. The son snitched on the Wilkes Mafia Family, but the Mafia could not touch the son because he was in witness protection program, so they got back by killing the preacher and his wife."

The story was eerily similar to the one Donnie Barrentine had allegedly told Jeff Kittrell in jail. The Swains had no son, but the caller seemed to be talking about Lawrence Brown. The caller didn't explain what the Wilkes Mafia Family was. But Barrentine's crew had connections to smugglers in Wilkes County, North Carolina. Frustratingly, the detectives couldn't ask more specific information because the tip was anonymous. But it did deepen their already very, very deep suspicions about Barrentine. In addition to Barrentine's alleged confessions, Lawrence Brown got his way in the Swains' estate, which turned out to be worth $50,000 in total. His stepdaughter, LaFane, won a legal battle with Harold Swain's surviving siblings—Harold was one of eighteen kids—to collect the money. Of course, the jailhouse informant hadn't mentioned anything about insurance money when he talked to Butch Kennedy. But people who knew the Swains and Brown were suspicious that Brown could have been involved. Could the attack have been to benefit Brown rather than to send him a message? Could the "send a message" story be a cover to make Brown seem innocent? Kennedy wanted so badly to understand how Brown could fit in with Barrentine, who walked free from federal prison a few days after the Swain murders hit national TV.

By the end of January 1989, the detectives had cleared eighty-eight leads from the show. They'd soon clear ten more. Then thirty-seven more. They were having flashbacks to the early days of the investigation: get a tip, clear a tip. The onslaught seemed endless. Kennedy would sit on his back porch after work and down a few Bud Lights to ease his angst. The chief deputy was always on call and couldn't get drunk even at night. So, Kennedy had just enough to feel a little lighter, just enough to keep going.

PART II

IN DARKENED WATER

———————— ~ ————————

When you look at the Satilla River, you don't see the Satilla River. The black water spreads out like a long sheet of glass, like a mirror showing everything above, but nothing below. As it creeps, you can see the blue sky on the water's surface, the pine trees lined up like soldiers on the bank, the kids flying off rope swings, sailing on the air until the splash. The reason for the reflection, essentially, is history. Vegetation—leaves, sticks, pine straw—falls to the riverbed and, because the water moves so achingly slowly, it sits there. Day by day, these small bits of life decay and release tannins that stain, like a tea bag diffusing through a pot of hot water, making it too dark to see through. But if you jump in and look under the surface, the illusion breaks.

10

On the Path

One day in early 1985, a fourteen-year-old Camden County High School freshman was drawing attention to himself in art class, singing. Mike Ellerson was a handsome athlete, already pushing six feet. Mike loved attention, and he was earning it in class, hoping to impress one girl in particular.

> *I can dream about you*
> *Oh, I can dream about you, whoa oh whoa*

Mike lived with his grandmother, a social worker who wanted him to attend Tuskegee University to become a lawyer. But Mike wasn't thinking about that kind of thing lately. Right now, as Mike mimicked Dan Hartman, bleeding himself dry over bouncy keys and slick guitar on the *Streets of Fire* soundtrack, he was thinking about the girl in art class. Soon, they'd start dating. He caught as many rides as he could to see her in Spring Bluff, which was nearly thirty miles away. He sneaked around to call her at night and prayed he wasn't running up his grandmother's phone bill.

One night that March, Mike couldn't find anyone to take him to Spring Bluff. But things were heating up and he'd find a way to see her. As it happened, Mike's mom, who lived across the street from her mother and Mike, had some friends over for drinks after work, and Mike noticed her car keys left unattended. He waited until everyone was warmed up and ignoring him. He snagged the keys and slipped outside into the waning daylight toward the Oldsmobile Cutlass in the driveway. Mike put the car in neutral and pushed it across a small field so that no one would hear it start. At the edge of the road, the fourteen-year-old climbed in the driver's seat, turned the key, and pressed on the gas.

He drove down side roads, then through the main drag in St. Marys. Cautiously, Mike plodded north on I-95. The sun dipped over the marshes and the tide shifted the waters of the Satilla River. A few hundred yards before he would've passed Rising Daughter Baptist Church, he turned down Spring Bluff Road.

For what felt like a long time, Mike and his girlfriend sat next to each other watching TV with her parents. *When are they going to bed?* Mike kept thinking. Around 9 p.m. there was a pounding on the kitchen door.

Oh shit, Mike said quietly to his girlfriend. *That's my mom.*

Your mom?

Yeah, I stole her car.

You stole a car?!

The girl's father, looking annoyed, answered the door. A woman entered. It wasn't Mike's mom. It was someone from the neighborhood, shouting in anguish: *Some white man came in the church and killed the Swains!*

Mike Ellerson wouldn't remember any of the rest of the exchange. Ringing in his head was the fact that a white man was riding around this neighborhood killing Black people like him. It had only been a few years since Atlanta's Black neighborhoods were terrorized by the kidnapping and murders of more than twenty children, nearly all boys. Mike's mom and grandmother, like so many adults, talked about it in hushed tones around the kids. In Mike's neighborhood and so many others, kids had to be home once the streetlights kicked on. Now a gunman in Spring Bluff?

Mike raced home down I-95. Was it ninety miles an hour? One hundred? He was too busy watching the rearview mirror. Every car behind him could have been the killer. He slowed down on the sleepy streets of St. Marys. He pushed the car back to the driveway in silence and walked home to his grandmother's house. Mike wouldn't tell his mother or grandmother that story until years later, once he'd become a Camden County sheriff's deputy.

AFTER HIGH SCHOOL, ELLERSON DIDN'T KNOW WHAT HE would do.

His older cousin knew the sheriff and encouraged Ellerson to ask about a job. Ellerson was called in for an interview to be a jailer in February 1991. Ellerson walked into the sheriff's office to hear two men— one white, one Black—hollering at each other. *You son of a bitch! Fuck you!* The fight was over allegations that jailers had beaten fourteen Black prisoners for fighting and causing trouble. Sheriff Smith denied that his jailers had beaten anyone but wouldn't allow visitors in to check on the prisoners.

Ellerson recognized the voice of the shouting Black man. It was Robert Cummings, head of the Camden County NAACP. To Mike, Cummings was a local hero. Ellerson was thinking about walking out when an officer called his name, offering to give him a tour.

The jail administrator showed Mike the control room for security and introduced him around. He pointed out the library, the kitchen, Medical, the laundry room. Mike wanted to ask his tour guide what Robert Cummings and the sheriff were hollering about in that back office, but it seemed like a sore subject. Walls gave way to glass as they entered the population area, where prisoners were locked behind heavy doors with small windows. Hearing a visitor, the men came to their doors, and some of them recognized Ellerson.

Come on, Mike, a voice said in heartbreak over Mike's apparent arrest. *Not you, not you.*

Aw, man, shouted another. *Mike's the police!*

And he was. He got the job. For a few days, he was nervous about working in a jail, particularly after he learned of the recent events there—prisoners had allegedly fought over what to watch on TV, then locked jailers out of the lounge, either to prevent punishment or in fear of the type of beatings by jailers that the men said ended up happening. But Ellerson looked around at the locked-up men and saw guys he'd played football with, had classes with, knew from around. He saw more than one of his cousins. He figured he'd be safe, but he had no idea how complicated it would be with Sheriff Bill Smith—the white man shouting at the NAACP leader—as his boss.

~

ON MARCH 13, 1992, STATE AND FEDERAL AGENTS RAIDED THE Camden County jail and Sheriff Bill Smith's home on the edge of the Crooked River. This was how Smith found out that he'd been under investigation for a year. Agents also raided the home of Smith's girlfriend—a niece of the notoriously corrupt McIntosh County sheriff Tom Poppell—and the jail administrator's house. A spokesman for the Georgia Attorney General's Office revealed to *The Atlanta Journal* that the investigation pertained to "use of inmate labor by a public official for personal gain, violation of court orders and oath of office, failure to serve warrants, criminal contempt, hindering prosecution of a felon, and other statutes."

Like sheriffs all over the state (and country), Smith used prisoners from the jail to do work around the county, typically landscaping. Prisoner labor was a regular sight all through the South: you'd see crews of men in matching jumpsuits picking up trash on the side of the road, pushing trash carts down courthouse hallways, and, in some cases, working farmland owned by the government. The jailed men and women who did these jobs were called trustees; the only difference between regular prisoners and trustees was that the trustees got to leave their cells to do odd jobs for the local government. But Smith pushed his trustee program further than most sheriffs. A former prison laborer said that he and other trustees washed cars, cleaned people's houses, and did laundry for the sheriff and his family. They worked on the sheriff's house. They even fed the hogs at the Ponderosa, Sheriff Smith's hideaway ranch.

Though he denied it, investigators believed that Smith wasn't paying the prisoners, which made it akin to forced labor. The former prisoner said that he and others were coerced into these projects by threats that if they didn't work, they'd no longer be trustees and would be barred from leaving the jail, which had been critical to their mental health while surviving incarceration. The same prisoner, who unsuccessfully sued Smith, had purportedly been given alcohol by the sheriff while working on Smith's home and then drunkenly crashed a county car he'd been allowed to drive alone. Years later, investigative journalists, activists, and scholars would demonstrate for mass audiences the horrors that others already knew: White officials, especially in the South, had used the thirteenth amendment, which prohibits slavery except as punishment for a crime, to re-enslave Black people after the Civil War. Even if the prisoners who sued Sheriff Smith didn't use these words to frame their experiences, the work they were doing was effectively forced labor. And they likely knew that Smith, a man descended from generations of small-town sheriffs, would be a hard man to bring to justice.

At Sheriff Smith's home in the high-dollar Harriett's Bluff area, agents took paint samples and gallons of paint, along with notes and letters. At his girlfriend's house, they confiscated a photo of the couple in the Bahamas, curious if he'd paid for the trip with drug money. When asked about the allegations, Smith told *The Atlanta Journal* that he was innocent and felt violated by the searches. "I can't believe this is happening," Smith said. He called the investigation political, the result of a vendetta against him. He questioned the timing, right as he was seeking reelection.

The last couple of years had been tumultuous at the sheriff's office. Kennedy and Gregory had recently investigated two I-95 deputies who'd been lying about how much drug money they'd seized while skimming thousands off the top. The sheriff had also been sued and held in contempt of court for declining to arrest a friend—a local doctor enamored with Confederate history—who had been charged with failing to pay alimony. Just a few months after the raid on the sheriff, one of Smith's highest-ranking and closest deputies was indicted for allegedly planting cocaine on suspects. Kennedy had to work on that case, which he feared would end his time at the sheriff's office. Smith was also upset that after seven years Kennedy still hadn't arrested the Swains' killer. Resentment had reached a tipping point.

In November 1992, the day after the sheriff won reelection, beating out a longtime officer who was a friend of Kennedy's, Kennedy cleaned out his office and walked away. Sheriff Smith thought it was time for Kennedy to resign, and Kennedy agreed. The job that once gave Kennedy's life meaning, that he'd gravitated toward because he wanted to help people like his dad had, was gone. Kennedy had officially failed to solve the Swains' murders. He sat up at night, thinking of how he'd let everyone down.

Joe Gregory was still working the case. But he was assigned to the regional GBI office, which meant he had investigations across a dozen counties. Each one took time from the Swain case. The case was badly stalled.

Meanwhile, Mike Ellerson was working his way up at the sheriff's office, impressing supervisors and getting more and more responsibility. Kennedy had been a mentor to Ellerson when he was a young investigator. Not long after watching the veteran lawman leave, Ellerson started to think more about the murders at Rising Daughter Baptist Church and that scary night fleeing down I-95, hoping the killer wasn't after him. Ellerson started to think that maybe he should be the one to give the case a fresh look.

11

Baton

Butch Kennedy took a job at the Camden County Tax Commissioner's Office where, as a Delinquent Tax Collector, he wore a polo shirt and munched on M&Ms he stashed in his new metal desk, which he rarely left. He thought of the Swain case every day. In his new job, when he got off work, he was just off—no emergency calls, no people to help. With the extra time, he found himself drinking more. You could find him many nights out on his back porch, cracking open Bud Lights and sitting in silence until he was ready to go to bed. Within months, Kennedy was divorced from Patsy. It was, Kennedy would admit, all his fault.

Kennedy clung to the hope that he and Gregory could still close the case. Gregory tried in the next few years to reinterview people connected to Donnie Barrentine. Kennedy went with him to speak with Jeff Kittrell again, but Kittrell said he couldn't give him anything new. Gregory and Kennedy had become battle-bonded, but now, separated from his sense of purpose, Kennedy felt more alone. All he saw were the disappointments.

Across Camden County, Sheriff Smith's influence was growing

as drug-related seizures ballooned. He found creative uses for the money and assets seized. Residents saw deputies riding in tricked-out sports cars that had been taken from alleged drug smugglers. Officers showed off the fancy cars to schoolchildren while urging them to "Just Say No" if anyone offered them drugs. Local churches and community were grateful for Smith's donations, even though they knew where the money came from. Sure, there were bad head-lines, but the sheriff's office was doing a lot to improve the Smith administration's reputation.

The yearslong investigation into the sheriff's office ended without charges against Sheriff Smith or anyone else. The sheriff continued using jail trustees for whatever kind of work he saw fit. GBI officials thought that Smith had broken the law. But the law they thought he broke—misuse of prisoner labor for personal gain—was merely a mis-demeanor. They could see the sheriff's defense now: the community would do well to focus on the wheelchair ramps the trustees built, the cemeteries they landscaped. Smith knew that his audience wasn't sympathetic to people accused of crimes. But investigators wondered: Would a jury really convict a sheriff in a case like this? In the same county that elected him? And his father? And his grandfather?

~

BY 1998, GREGORY WAS WORKING LESS AND LESS ON THE CASE. AS he approached retirement, he'd started focusing on crime scene inves-tigation. One day he was dispatched to a possible homicide at the naval base. He was driving there in a large white GBI van on I-95 when a tire blew. The van cut to the right, veering off the side of the road. Gregory tried to brace himself as the vehicle rolled four, five, six times. His tall frame jostled around the cab as it tumbled.

When the rolling finally stopped, Gregory checked himself.

He could move. He crawled out of the busted window on his hands and knees.

A nurse who was headed to work pulled over. She saw Gregory crawling, trying to get up.

You lay down and don't move, she ordered.

He complied. The pain set in—it surrounded him more than he could've imagined was possible. He'd seen numerous injured and dead people in his career, but he'd never been the subject of the life-or-death emergency. Later, in the hospital, he would learn that he had broken many bones in his back and neck and dislocated his shoulder.

Gregory's career was over. But very soon, a new generation would take the baton and begin seeking closure for the case that had haunted Camden County for over a decade.

MIKE ELLERSON HAD WORKED HIS WAY UP TO DETECTIVE AT THE sheriff's office. His cases were typically burglaries, thefts, or drug sales. He didn't work many homicides, but he knew that no one was on the Swain case. He told his supervisor he wanted to start looking into it. The crime had stuck with Ellerson since he was fourteen. It seemed fitting that a detective, particularly a Black one, with a vivid memory of that awful night could possibly be the one to unravel the case. It had been cold, without a detective assigned to it, for years. Ellerson's supervisor said to go ahead when he had extra time.

Ellerson started reviewing the file—nine volumes in three-ringed binders filled with thirteen years of work and hundreds of leads. As Ellerson flipped through the weathering pages, he found the names of people he wanted to talk to, made notes of things to explore. He read about Donnie Barrentine and the drug smugglers. He read about Erik Sparre claiming that he'd killed the "n ——— s in that church." He read the tips about Dennis Perry trying to shut Harold Swain up about a field of marijuana Swain allegedly found. The case was daunting. Ellerson had seen how Gregory and Kennedy, two men he respected, had worked to unravel this for so long. But Ellerson rarely hurt for confidence.

At about the same time, after the prison labor lawsuit and the yearslong investigation, there were rumblings that Sheriff Smith might finally face serious opposition in the 2000 election from a local Black civic leader. Smith had relied on the Black vote. It was getting harder to run as a Democrat and win as conservative white voters were fleeing en masse to the Republican Party. Smith also knew the trouble that his scandals had caused. While he passed out money, his legal fees were expensive for county taxpayers.

Facing these converging liabilities, Smith, who had considered Harold Swain a friend, decided it was time the Swain case got a fresh examination. He didn't choose Ellerson to lead. Instead, the sheriff used I-95 drug money to hire a former deputy, Dale Bundy, and assigned him to work on the Swain murders full-time for one year, with no guarantee of a job after that. Bundy was hired for $28,500 with the funds, of course, coming from Smith's big bag of dope money. Bundy's employment contract called him a cold case investigator who would work on investigations that had been stalled for more than five years, but the understanding was that he was there specifically to solve the Swain murders. Ellerson was informed he would assist Bundy. He was gutted. The case meant so much to him. He had worked on as many or more homicides as Bundy, and Ellerson had solved another murder just a year earlier—a tough case that ended up being profoundly personal and, a lot of people thought, showed Ellerson's character and investigative prowess. Meanwhile, Bundy had most recently worked in IT. But Bundy was a known entity to Sheriff Smith, someone he thought could get the job done.

Bundy came from the McCarthy family, big landowners in Camden County who hosted rich and powerful people for bird hunts and political fundraisers. Still sporting the angular military-style haircut to prove it, he'd been a police officer in the Coast Guard. Bundy had graduated at the top of his police academy class but resigned from his position as jail administrator over frustrations with repeated escapes, which he didn't think Sheriff Smith was committed to stopping. Still, he hadn't been on bad terms with the sheriff personally. In fact, his daughter worked in Sheriff Smith's office.

BUNDY STARTED WORK ON THE CASE ON JULY 1, 1998. HE COULD count himself among a growing number of detectives across the United States whose job it was to solve crimes that had previously stumped investigators. The crack epidemic—and officials' abject failure in addressing the public health and safety crisis it caused—contributed to soaring homicide tallies in the late 1980s and early 1990s. But by the late 1990s, the bloodshed had slowed. This left many police departments with fewer serious cases to contend with; they could turn their attention to ones that had previously stalled. At the same time, police were gaining new tools to solve old crimes: DNA testing, national fingerprint databases, and enhanced crime scene processing. DNA had freed scores of innocent people from prison and helped solve numerous cold cases. Many detectives were also discovering that the passage of time helped witnesses overcome apprehensions about telling what they knew.

Cold case detectives were putting up impressive numbers. In New York City, the cold case squad said it cleared more than two hundred cases in less than three years. Detectives in Washington, DC, cleared more than a hundred. New Orleans said its cold case unit found answers in one hundred crimes within just a couple of years. But as much promise as these investigations showed, cold cases had terrible complications built in.

Time faded witnesses' memories. Some witnesses and suspects had died. Physical evidence was sometimes lost. People who ended up suspects were at a terrible disadvantage in defending themselves because of the difficulty in constructing their alibis. It might be easy enough to remember, or even find evidence, that you went to bed at 9:30 p.m. last Friday. It might be basically impossible to figure out when you fell asleep one Friday night ten years ago in the 1980s.

The thirteen years that had passed since Harold and Thelma Swain were killed had not been kind to the investigation. The witnesses were aging, and some were in failing health. Physical evidence was missing—a lot of physical evidence. Into the void, Bundy and Ellerson stepped.

Bundy's first task was to review the monstrous case file that Ellerson had already studied. Bundy tore through it in six days. He came away wondering if the witnesses from the church had heard anything since the murders. He decided to try reconnecting with them.

DECEMBER 5, 1997. A FRIDAY NIGHT IN WOODBINE, GEORGIA.

Mike Ellerson was the first investigator on scene. He made his way inside a rural home where a forty-one-year-old man lay motionless on the kitchen floor. Sandy Myers was bloodied from a single fatal gunshot to the chest. Myers was a friend of Ellerson's mom and a former sheriff's deputy who, according to rumors, had gotten involved in drugs sales. Ellerson had seen Sandy at his mom's birthday party a week earlier, laughing and joking. At the crime scene, Ellerson stood over Myers for a moment, not realizing that his tears were falling on Sandy's chest.

Ellerson and other officers quickly found witnesses in the area and learned the name of the suspected killer: Rodriguez "Rico" Hamilton. He was Ellerson's brother, who also knew the victim. Mike and Rico grew up together, but they weren't close as adults. Ellerson was a deputy, and Hamilton was in the drug trade. Witnesses and evidence from the scene pointed to his brother as the killer. Ellerson was shocked that his brother would do such a thing. Caught up in the moment and furious at his brother, Ellerson didn't think to turn the case over to someone who didn't share blood with the possible killer. Blood was one thing. Killing a man was another. Ellerson started plotting with other officers about where to find Hamilton until supervisors said he couldn't arrest his own brother and removed him from the case. Ellerson called Hamilton and convinced him to turn himself in, demanding that he do it or Ellerson would physically drag him to the sheriff's office—dead or alive. Just a few months later, Ellerson decided to turn his intensity to the Swain case.

12

Cold Shoulder Day

Dale Bundy didn't want to cause the witnesses any unnecessary stress. He knew the women might be afraid. He thought they might be a bit leery of law enforcement, too. Bundy decided to be discreet, donning blue jeans and a casual shirt instead of his uniform, and he opted to drive his personal car to the first witness's house.

Cora Fisher was sixty-six and in declining health. She had retired from her job in housekeeping at the Holiday Inn. In the years since the gunman had shown up at Rising Daughter, she remained tormented by the knowledge that he had gotten away. Fisher had always said she got a good look at the man before fainting. But when Bundy showed up at her house one July afternoon, Fisher was hesitant to talk. The detective, seven days into his investigation, figured he could work his way up to the hard questions. With witnesses and suspects alike, Bundy spoke softly in a disarming tone, almost as if he was apologizing for asking questions. That is, unless he thought he was being misled. His tone could change then.

As they sat on her porch, Bundy went over Fisher's original statement, which was that she'd seen the killer's face as he struggled with

Harold Swain and that the man had turned the gun toward Fisher just before she fainted. Fisher confirmed her statement for Bundy. But Bundy had a feeling that Fisher was holding back.

Cora, Bundy finally said, *do you think you know who killed Harold and Thelma Swain?*

I don't think anything, she said. *I know who killed Harold and Thelma Swain.*

Fisher said she'd known for a decade who did it but was afraid to come forward. Shortly after *Unsolved Mysteries* aired in 1988, a white woman she didn't know came to Fisher's house with a photograph of a man. When Fisher saw that picture, the flash of recognition nearly caused her to faint. She told Bundy the man in that photo was the killer.

I'm positive.

Bundy could feel the world stop as he listened. He asked who the man was.

Fisher wouldn't say. She said she was too scared. She'd seen him, she explained, at least three times in the years after the murders. He parked near her home and just stared. It seemed he wanted her to know he was watching, that he was waiting to kill her the moment she opened her mouth about him to the police. Fisher refused to say his name or the name of the white woman who showed her the photo. All she would tell Bundy was that the killer's grandfather lived on Dover Bluff Road, not far from the church, and that the white woman lived in a mobile home on the highway next to Rising Daughter Baptist.

IN SUMMER, THE GRASS AND WEEDS GET WILD ALONG HIGHWAY 17. With the intense humidity and temperatures regularly hitting 100 degrees, it gives the sense that you're traveling through the jungle except for the pine trees flanking the road. Luckily for Bundy, he didn't have to sweat through his shirt very long before he found a yellow trailer about a half mile from Rising Daughter.

The woman who opened the door listened as Bundy explained that he was investigating the murders of Harold and Thelma Swain and looking for someone who'd shown witnesses a photo.

Well, she said, *it took you long enough to find me, come in and I will tell you what you need to know to make your case.*

Jane Beaver was fifty-nine and from Spring Bluff. She had been in the Air National Guard and then worked two decades in the accounting department at a coastal scientific research facility. Laid off seven years earlier in 1991, she started a home business, Ceramics by Jane. Ceramics was a meditative craft, good for a woman who had been through hell.

She sat Bundy down in her home, crowded with cats, and didn't hesitate. She told him she knew who the killer was: Dennis Perry. Perry had dated her daughter before the murders. They broke up, she said, but he stopped by their home about three weeks before the shooting, in February 1985. Beaver described a strange visit. Perry had on a pair of women's glasses and was putting on an effeminate voice, joking around. Then the conversation meandered to Harold Swain. Perry said he intended to kill him. The reason, Beaver said, was that Perry had asked Swain to borrow money, and Swain had laughed in his face.

Beaver's daughter, Carol Anne, wasn't there on the day Bundy visited. The young couple had split after Perry broke his back falling from a tree stand while deer hunting and moved to the Atlanta area to live with his mother and recuperate. They couldn't make the 260-mile distance work, but they stayed friendly. Perry had never been close to his ex's mom, but for whatever reason, Jane Beaver said, he told her he intended to kill Harold Swain. *I'm going to kill that n———*, she quoted him saying. She said she'd asked Perry about the Swains' murders after it happened. He laughed and walked away. Bundy couldn't believe what he was hearing. How could Kennedy and Gregory have missed this?

~

VANZOLA WILLIAMS STARED AT THE PICTURE OF DENNIS PERRY: a young man with shoulder-length hair playing with a baby on the floor, looking up into the camera.

Bundy and Ellerson had stopped by Williams's house. Ellerson was Bundy's in, because he knew Williams and had gone to school with her granddaughter, but he was still frustrated to have been demoted to helper. Ellerson was surprised to learn that they were investigating Dennis Perry. Ellerson remembered reading about Perry's alibi in the case files: he'd worked until early evening near Atlanta on the day of the murders, which meant he couldn't possibly have made it to the church in time to commit the murders. Ellerson assumed that Bundy had read that too, but Ellerson didn't know that Bundy didn't trust the original detectives' work, although he'd learn it later. For now, Ellerson hung by the door, paying close attention as Bundy asked Williams if the man in the picture was the killer.

Williams, nearing seventy, tried to summon the face she'd seen just once in the vestibule's dim lighting thirteen years ago. Was the man in this family photo, holding a beaming toddler, really the killer?

Ellerson was trying not to disrespect the new head of the investigation by harping on it, but he didn't understand why Bundy just brought the one photo. Protocol was to offer a group of different faces. Showing Williams one photo sent an obvious message that Bundy thought Perry might be guilty. If he let her see five or six photos, she would have no idea who the detective was investigating, and an identification would be much more powerful. But Bundy figured protocol didn't matter because Williams had already been shown this same photo of Perry and, according to Beaver, said he was the killer.

Williams said regretfully that she just couldn't be sure if this photo was of the shooter. But she agreed that this man looked like the killer, and Bundy found that compelling.

AS THE COLD CASE INVESTIGATION PROGRESSED, DENNIS PERRY was living outside Jacksonville, Florida, working as a framer on a construction crew and building his own carpentry business. Most of Perry's work was on a nearby island, only accessible by barge. It was often slow to arrive, and that was fine by him. Perry fished while waiting nearly every day, as he had when he was growing up near the Little Satilla River with his grandparents in Spring Bluff.

One day in August 1998, Bundy showed up at the Perrys' house.

I'm with the Camden County Sheriff's Office, Bundy said to Perry's wife, Karen.

Are you here about the murders?

He thought it was suspicious she would need so little information to know why a police officer from Georgia had just appeared at their door. But Karen had an explanation. She and Dennis had seen the old *Unsolved Mysteries* episode. It frequently aired as a rerun. Though it didn't mention Perry, the episode prompted him to tell his wife that he'd briefly been considered a suspect in 1988 but was innocent. She had no doubt he was telling her the truth. She figured she'd have known by then if her husband of seven years was that coldhearted.

When Perry arrived home from work, he spoke with Bundy in the driveway. Perry reiterated his alibi: He was in the Atlanta area when the murders happened. He said he knew of Harold Swain but didn't personally know him. He said he would never commit such a terrible crime. He didn't even own a handgun. Then he mentioned a detail that

Bundy found significant—that Swain had the large hands of a pulp-wooder. It was well-known around Spring Bluff that Swain had owned and operated a pulpwood business, and that fact was mentioned often in news coverage of the murders. But it isn't clear how Swain's hands came up in the interview from the one-paragraph summary Bundy wrote months later.

After a few minutes, Bundy ended the interview and left Dennis and Karen Perry to wonder what to make of the detective's visit. It was certainly unnerving. But Perry remembered when Kennedy and Gregory had cleared him over a decade ago; the investigation caused stress for a few weeks at most. He figured Bundy would move on now that Perry had explained his alibi.

Ellerson parked at the sheriff's office, amid ancient oaks with Spanish moss strung limb to limb like Christmas lights. He had a meeting that day with Bundy and other investigators. They planned to talk through the church murders, to brainstorm and weigh theories. They gathered around a table in the squad room. Ellerson listened uncomfortably as others went over the evidence about Dennis Perry.

Finally, after someone asked what he thought about Perry, Ellerson said he didn't think the evidence was there. He had seen the documents indicating that Perry worked late in Atlanta on the day of the murders. Perry couldn't have made it to the church by 8 or 9 p.m., especially since he didn't have a car. Ellerson didn't care what anybody said— Butch Kennedy and Joe Gregory had cleared Perry. Ellerson trusted their work. Ellerson had another suspect in mind: Donnie Barrentine.

Ellerson's warning was met with awkward silence that spoke volumes: this investigation was done with that outlandish Donnie Barrentine–Lawrence Brown theory. Ellerson would come to call this Cold Shoulder Day. From that day forward, Bundy stopped asking him for help. As the case moved further from him, Mike Ellerson told a coworker he was glad he had nothing to do with it. *That's gonna come back to haunt them*, he said.

⁓

ON THE DAY BEFORE THANKSGIVING 1998, A WOMAN CONTACTED the sheriff's office, saying she had information about the murders. More than a decade after the shooting, tips were rare—and this one was big. Bundy and a GBI agent went to interview her at the mobile home park she helped run near Brunswick. Rhonda Minder was soft-spoken but tough, hardened after surviving harrowing domestic violence. For about a decade, Minder had been afraid to tell authorities what she was about to say. But she finally had resolved to speak up. Minder was the second ex-wife of Erik Sparre, the purported racist who admitted to committing the murders on tape in 1986. Kennedy and Gregory dropped him as a suspect because of his alibi that he was stocking shelves at a Brunswick grocery store all night.

Minder, who married Sparre shortly after the murders and his split from Emily Head, remembered when police arrived at his parents' home with a search warrant during the Swain case. Sparre watched them approach through the window. *They're not gonna take me*, he said.

Minder also recalled one moment in 1988 when Sparre had her pinned down on the bed with a pillow over her face.

Don't kill me! she screamed, muffled.

She fought free and blurted out, *You could have killed those people in Camden County.*

Yeah, I could have killed those people.

That counted as the second time Sparre allegedly suggested that he was, or could have been, the Swains' killer. The GBI agent took terse notes of the meeting, and he didn't say what he and Bundy made of the woman's information. Sparre had an alibi in the case file and that made it easy enough to disregard what Minder said. Bundy moved his focus back to Dennis Perry. Bundy felt like he was making progress with that lead, and Sheriff Smith had just hired him full-time, indefinitely instead of the one year he was initially hired for.

Plus, the detective had one eyewitness identifying Perry as the killer and another saying he looked like the killer. Another witness said Perry told her he intended to kill Harold Swain. But Bundy still didn't know how Perry could've traveled—if he hadn't been working—from the Atlanta area to Spring Bluff without a car. He turned to Perry's family in hopes of shaking loose new information.

Bundy met Perry's mother, Helen, at her home outside Savannah. She told Bundy that her son was living with her when the murders happened and working near Atlanta. She explained that he'd hurt his back in a fall in December 1984 and moved in with her after a week in the hospital. He'd been easing back into work and took a job at a concrete company. Helen said it was April or May—weeks after the March 11 murders—when her son visited Spring Bluff for the first time after hurting his back. She remembered renting him a car from Hertz for the trip. There was something else, Helen told Bundy, that they needed to consider: her son wasn't a violent person. He was congenial and outgoing and had trouble with anxiety.

"They may have thought Dennis was there," his mother said, "but I promise you he was not."

PERRY AND HIS LOVED ONES WERE TRYING TO ANSWER A CRITICAL question: Where was Perry on the night of the murders after leaving work? In 1985, people typically left little in the way of paper trails in their daily lives. There weren't time-stamped emails or voicemails. When Gregory first looked at Perry as a suspect in 1988, Perry's boss said he'd worked into the early evening near Atlanta. Yet Bundy said that there was nothing in the Swain murders investigation case file about the interview with the boss.

Perry thought he remembered the night in question. On March 11, 1985, Perry's friend forgot to give his mom her birthday gift, and with Perry and his brother tagging along, they dropped it off to her that night. The Perry brothers both remembered the late birthday gift, as did the friend's mother. She recalled the trio showing up at her home at 8:30 p.m., falling over drunk and giggling, presenting her with a coatrack. Her home was in Jonesboro, more than two hundred miles from Rising Daughter Baptist, where the killer entered the church at roughly the same time.

Donna Nash, the friend's mother, was firm to the police that she recalled this, and she was clear where she stood on the investigation.

"I can tell you right now: Dennis Perry would not harm a hair on anyone's head," Nash told a pair of GBI agents in September 1999, "and he is not a racist."

The agents weren't moved.

It turned out Perry and others had been confused about the date of the murders. Nash's birthday was actually the night *before* the murders, which tanked the late-gift alibi.

ON JANUARY 13, 2000, AT 4:15 P.M., BUNDY MET IN JACKSONVILLE with local law enforcement and agents with the US Marshal's Service in the parking lot of a Sam's Club. That morning, a grand jury had indicted Perry on two counts of murder. There was a warrant for his arrest. The plan was to pull him over as he drove home from work.

They waited off the side of Sawpit Road, the only way into his neighborhood.

At 6:22 p.m., one of the officers spotted a black 1988 Ford F-150 pickup—Perry's truck.

Perry, who had spent the last year and a half trying not to worry about the investigation, heard a siren and pulled over. An officer told him to get out of the truck and onto his knees with his hands in the air. Perry obliged.

Dennis, it's Detective Bundy. Just relax. You have the right to remain silent. Anything you say can be used against you. You're entitled to have a lawyer now and have him present now or at any time during questioning.

Perry couldn't take the words in. How could Bundy think he killed the Swains? How could Bundy think he would kill anyone?

Perry was taken to an interrogation room, surrounded by three investigators. He told them firmly that he was nowhere near Camden County on the night of the murders. He thought this was all a misunderstanding that he could help clear up, so he chose not to ask for a lawyer. The police decided not to record the interrogation. Instead, a GBI agent, who had a recorder on him, took notes, which is a far less efficient and far less accurate method of memorializing interviews. This would be a problem. Because the officer's notes claimed that Perry managed to make things much worse for himself.

"Perry stated he does remember drinking a lot and using drugs and cannot remember a lot about what happened."

"[The GBI agent] asked Perry if the gun went off by accident and Perry stated yes."

"[A Florida officer] asked Perry if he could put everything back together that happened, to make it right, would he, and Perry stated yes."

"Detective Bundy asked Perry if he was scared this day had been coming for a long time and Perry stated yes."

At this point Perry got scared.

"Perry stated, 'You're trying to put words in my mouth.'"

Perry felt ambushed, like the officers were feeding him a story. He realized he made a terrible mistake not asking for an attorney. He was bewildered, starting to panic, too afraid to say another word. The officers asked if he would make a statement on tape. He declined.

13

Facing Death

Joe Gregory learned that an arrest had been made in a phone call from his son, Tommy, who worked at the sheriff's office as a deputy.

Dad, you're not gonna believe this, Bundy actually made an arrest in the Swain case.

Who's the suspect? Joe asked, stunned.

Dennis Perry.

Who was Dennis Perry? Joe couldn't place him. But he was thrilled to know the case had been solved.

Gregory called Kennedy to see if he'd heard. The old friends were talking excitedly when Gregory finally placed Perry's name. He was, Gregory recalled, the man who had been in the Atlanta area working with the concrete company, the man Gregory and Kennedy eliminated as a suspect after his name came up in two leads, both from a notorious local fabulist.

Butch, we put his photo in a lineup, Gregory said.

Kennedy remembered. They'd done a photo spread for Vanzola Williams to make sure she didn't recognize Perry in 1988, and she hadn't. Kennedy felt sick. This wasn't the murderer.

Perry had been in jail for a month before his family was allowed to see him. In the first visit, Daniel Perry gave his younger brother a Men's Study Bible, the kind with homework questions in the margins. He was worried for Dennis's sanity.

On the back of the cover, Dennis wrote the date: February 11, 2000.

He was in Glynn County jail in Brunswick, which officials figured would limit the number of his fellow prisoners who might remember the murders at Rising Daughter. He worried he could be in trouble with other men if they found out what he'd been accused of. But Perry found that most men didn't ask what others were in for. They knew the allegations might be false. He had a work detail. When the other men went to sleep at night, Perry and his bunkmate would clean the dorms, which earned them an extra thirty minutes of TV time. They watched Jay Leno, David Letterman, and the nightly news.

Perry stayed informed on what was in the papers, too. The church murders were still big news. In *The Tribune & Georgian*, the Swains' niece, Cynthia Clayton, who'd been assured of Perry's guilt by authorities, said she was thankful. An editorial cartoon praised the investigation. It featured Smith and Bundy in a boat named SEIZED DRUG MONEY. Bundy is reeling in a big-eyed fish labeled SUSPECT IN A 15-YEAR-OLD MURDER CASE while the sheriff grins, holding the net.

Perry was devastated to know what people must be thinking of him. He had no record of violence and was horrified at the mere idea of taking a life, let alone two—especially in a church. He hated that people thought he was a killer, and it made it worse to think that they also probably thought he was a racist. He'd been around Black people all his life, and he loved the communities he'd lived in. He was determined to prove that the cops had him wrong, that he was innocent.

Perry tried to keep himself busy until the trial, reading his Bible and imagining his day in court. Perry had not been a religious man before his arrest. But he'd grown up in Georgia, where even if you don't go to church, a little sneaks in through the blinds. Now in jail, he found hope in the story of Job, a man who loses everything in a test of his faith to God, a man who holds on and is rewarded with more than he'd lost. Perry savored the words.

THE OUTLAWS WERE GETTING OLD. SOME WERE GETTING OUT after long prison sentences for running cannabis and cocaine. They once toted machine guns and flew clandestine international flights, bribed cops and threatened rivals. Now they shuttled children to school and T-ball practice. They repented and tried to stay on the right side of probation and parole officers.

Donnie Barrentine, long free from the federal penitentiary, was settling into a small plot of land near Marianna, Florida, his Panhandle hometown. His old life was fading into memory. He missed it. He even missed federal prison sometimes because of all the friends he'd had to leave behind. But for all the war stories Donnie could tell, there was sadness, too. His cousin Greg Barrentine, who'd gone to federal prison in a separate case, had lost two children to accidental shootings—a son and a daughter who fell victim to playing with guns that adults had left in reach.

Though police in Florida had suspected Donnie Barrentine in various shootings, he was never charged. He maintained his innocence in every case, including the Swain murders—just as he would if Dale Bundy approached him. But a couple of years into the renewed investigation, Bundy hadn't contacted Barrentine or shown interest in him as a suspect. Then Perry's defense attorney found out about the Donnie Barrentine–Lawrence Brown theory that the original detectives had developed: that the Swains ended up dead because gang members tied to Barrentine's crew wanted to send a message to their niece's husband, Lawrence Brown. The thinking was that Brown owed money he wasn't paying or had started snitching. After learning of these allegations, Perry's attorney protested in "amazement" to the DA's office that the state was ignoring the evidence against Barrentine.

THE DEFENSE COMPLAINT CAUSED ENOUGH CONCERN AT THE DA's office that Bundy soon headed to Florida. He needed to speak with the man who'd first alerted Kennedy and Gregory to Barrentine's alleged statements about the murders. Bundy found Jeff Kittrell at the Panhandle grocery store where he worked when he wasn't preaching at a nearby church. Kittrell, Barrentine's codefendant in the 1985 machine gun case, went through his story again. He said there was a party a few weeks after the church murders where Barrentine claimed he was God because he could take life and that he'd taken the lives of two Black people in a church.

Bundy had been scrutinizing Barrentine's past and found patterns in the allegations against him: When Barrentine was said to have done a shooting, it was normally well calculated, with a plan to leave no witnesses. The shootings usually involved a shotgun, not a small-caliber handgun like the one used in the Swains' murder.

"I'm not calling you a liar, don't misunderstand me," Bundy told Kittrell, the chaotic sounds of the grocery store behind them. "I think it was Donnie shooting off his mouth about something he'd seen on the news. Because there's some things that you've told us, right here, things just don't add up."

Bundy said he could "get Donnie Barrentine off the hook for this one."

This was, to say the least, not how detectives tended to respond

when a witness offered up a murder suspect. But Bundy would've had
to disregard Perry as a suspect to believe that Barrentine was guilty.
Barrentine had spoken of a friend's involvement in the murders, but
there was no evidence or allegation that Perry and Barrentine even
knew each other.

"The way this shooting was done is not Donnie Barrentine's style,"
Bundy told Kittrell. "This was done sloppily."

AS IS TYPICAL, PERRY'S TEAM WAS LOOKING INTO THE WIT-
nesses against him to get a fuller picture of who they were and where
they were coming from. Of particular interest was Jane Beaver. She
was the star witness in this case, the one who told Dale Bundy that
Perry told her he planned to kill Harold Swain. Her testimony was the
connective tissue that held the state's case together. And very quickly,
Perry's team started hearing stories about Beaver. People who knew
her said she had lost touch with reality. One of Perry's attorneys sent
a subpoena to the Georgia Department of Human Resources, saying
that Jane Beaver's mental health hospitalization history was of critical
importance because she was a key witness in a capital murder case. He
requested medical records from her recent hospitalizations in the hope
of understanding her state of mind. An assistant state attorney general wrote back on behalf of the health department, saying it couldn't
produce such records, if they existed, "because they are confidential,
and are not subject to discovery." As the trial neared, Perry's attorneys
tried a more direct approach in a new request for her hospitalization
records: "Jane Beaver is known and referred to by friends and family
members as 'Crazy Jane.' "

Georgia's health department offered Perry's team just one page,
disclosing that she'd been hospitalized for two months in 1991 with

a diagnosis of "Adjustment Disorder with Physical Complications." That was vague; it wouldn't do much for the defense. Prosecutors, however, may have known something about Beaver's mental state that they were keeping secret. On the state's copy of the motion seeking Beaver's mental health records, someone wrote a note in pen: "Suffered from delusional problems—hallucinations—paranoia."

Perry had heard stories about Beaver long before she accused him of murder. The more he heard through updates from his attorneys and family, the more Perry couldn't understand why he was sitting in jail without bond based on her word. He especially couldn't understand why he had to wait so long for the trial. He was stunned when he hit the first anniversary behind bars. Years two and three in jail were like slow-motion steamrollers trying to flatten his spirit. He was careful not to discuss his case on the phone, fearing that authorities who recorded all jail calls would use his words against him. He was still processing their most recent message: the DA's office wanted to send him to death row. Perry tried to reassure himself that they'd have to convict him to kill him, and he believed that any reasonable jury of twelve would hear the evidence and conclude that he was an innocent man.

As Perry's trial approached, the state offered him a deal. If he pled guilty to voluntary manslaughter, prosecutors would seek a ten-year sentence with credit for the three years he'd already spent in jail. The DA's office wasn't going easy on Perry to be nice; it was a sign that prosecutors feared that the jury wouldn't convict him. The offer was a rare show of weakness by the lead prosecutor in the case, John B. Johnson III, a man who viewed his pursuit of people accused of crimes—especially murders—as a divine calling. Ten years was an extraordinarily lenient offer for any double murder case, let alone a case prosecuted by Johnson. In 1977, in his first murder trial, he'd sent a seventeen-year-old convicted killer to death row and felt personally satisfied after watching the state execute him in the electric chair. The sentence Johnson offered Perry was more akin to the time you'd get for robbing a gas station without shooting anyone. Perry could take the deal and avoid risking his life in court. Still, Perry was hoping for an acquittal. He didn't want to plead guilty to something he insisted he didn't do, even if it meant risking a death sentence.

14

Surprises

When John Johnson rose to greet the jury on February 10, 2003, it had been nearly eighteen years since the murders. If it had been bold to charge a man fifteen years later, a capital trial after almost two decades without physical evidence was almost unheard of. But the prosecutor was known to push the limits, for winning cases that others thought were too weak to earn a conviction.

In his opening statement, he recalled the story of the Swains' murders in his methodical way. Most plot points—the white man in the vestibule, the blood on the church floor—were familiar territory from *Unsolved Mysteries*. But Johnson's story differed in significant ways. First and foremost, unlike the show years earlier, Johnson had no interest in Donnie Barrentine as a suspect in the case. Johnson's killer was Dennis Perry, and he was a coldhearted one. According to Johnson, Perry planned to kill Harold Swain and even fired a shot at Cora Fisher before she fainted. He didn't mention that Kennedy and Gregory had searched and found no evidence of a shot fired toward Fisher, but Kennedy and Gregory weren't the heroes of this story; they were merely foils. They were the cops who hadn't taken tips about Perry seriously enough. Dale Bundy was the hero detective in this story, the man who did what the original cops didn't: claim justice for the Swains.

In his opening statement, Perry's attorney, Dale Westling, told the jury another story, that the state's evidence didn't add up. He reminded them that detectives cleared Perry in 1988, when his alibi checked out and a key witness—Vanzola Williams—hadn't recognized his photo three years after the murders. Westling told the jury how that photo, along with the glasses found at the crime scene and nearly all the physical evidence, had disappeared and that the sheriff's office couldn't explain why.

Vanzola Williams took the stand. She was seventy-three. She'd told her story of encountering the man in the vestibule many times, but this was the day that had always been coming, the day when finally a jury hears. With luck, it would be the last time she ever had to speak about this again.

Johnson held a family photo of Dennis Perry.

"The person in this photograph," Johnson said, "do you recognize that person?"

"Yes."

"That was the man that was there that night?"

"Yes."

Just as she had when Bundy and Ellerson went to her home, Williams was more precise when given the opportunity.

"I can't say for sure that he was the man," she said. "He looked like the man that night."

CORA FISHER, SIXTY-NINE, WAS TOO ILL TO ATTEND THE TRIAL, so transcripts of her testimony were read into the record. It was awkward. It was also dramatic and confounding, as Fisher's story shifted throughout the transcript. She gave numerous details she hadn't when she was interviewed only hours after the shooting. One of the biggest discrepancies: she said now that when Harold Swain first saw the killer, he said, "Boy, what are you doing here?" She hadn't said that in the hours after the murders, and no other witness had reported a similar statement. Best as the others could tell that night, Swain didn't seem to know the man. But Fisher said she remembered it. In fact, Fisher said *she* recognized the killer when she saw him; she said that they locked eyes and he smiled. He was pointing the handgun right at her before she fainted. She said she'd intentionally not told Butch Kennedy or other investigators about this after the murders.

"Was there a reason," Johnson asked, "why you didn't tell them?"

"Yep."

"What was the reason?"

"My life," said Fisher.

Johnson asked if she remembered when Bundy showed her the photo of Perry that she'd recognized him and nearly fainted. She said she didn't remember, that her trauma had caused her to faint many times. "I've fallen so many times, because every time I would see somebody white coming at me with long hair or any kind of hair, I'd just swoop," Fisher said. Another surprise came when Fisher said that Perry went to school with her son, even though Perry was much younger than her sons.

Dale Westling, trying to tread gently, drew more conflicting statements from Fisher. He had an idea to test Fisher's memory and the strength of her identification of Dennis Perry as the killer. He handed her Defense Exhibit 1, which was a photo of a young white man with long hair. He made sure she put on her glasses before she examined the face.

"Does that look like the boy?" the attorney asked, referring to the killer.

"Yes, sir," she said. "They look the same to me."

The photo was of Donnie Barrentine.

At the defense table, Perry was trying to figure out what was happening, why Fisher was all over the place. The state had presented only two witnesses who didn't seem damning. Fisher was telling stories that she'd never told before and appeared confused; that had to go against her credibility. Perry's sister-in-law, who was the only relative allowed to watch the trial because the others were potential witnesses, debriefed with the others outside the courtroom: *There's no way he's getting convicted.* And next up was the woman known by some friends as "Crazy Jane."

Perry's friends and family knew a lot about Beaver's troubles. She'd had a life no one would envy: her first daughter died, and the toddler's father went to prison for murdering the child; and in 1976, her fifteen-year-old son died by suicide. She'd lost her job in accounting twelve years before Perry's trial, and she'd seemed to spiral since then. As much as people felt sorry for her, she could be explosive with paranoia that caused her to make wild accusations. Perry's supporters didn't understand that the jury wouldn't hear any context about Beaver's troubles. They could try to bring up her traumatic life, but without detailed hospitalization records explaining the apparent impact of her trauma, it could seem to the jury like a mean-spirited attack. Instead, Perry's team hoped that Beaver, the prosecution's star witness, would make it obvious in her testimony that she wasn't credible.

After she took the oath and gave her name for the record, Beaver appeared poised and offered a compelling—if brand new—story. Even Perry's attorney had never heard most of it, which wasn't how a trial was supposed to work. Beaver told the court that she saw the composite sketch in the newspaper and called the sheriff's office in 1985.

"Do you know who you talked to?" Johnson asked.

"No, I do not."

"What did you tell them?"

"I told them I wanted to speak with them because I'd had a conversation with a young man, that I thought they needed to check him out."

"Did anyone come visit you at that time?"

"No, they did not."

Beaver said she called five or six times, and no one ever called her back. There was no record of her calling once, but the jury had already heard that some records were missing. Then Beaver described how she'd visited Cora Fisher one day in the early 1990s.

"I told her that I had a conversation with him at my house and I had some pictures I would like for her just to look at," Beaver went on.

Beaver said Fisher immediately reacted to seeing Perry's face.

"She fell to the floor, and she was moaning. I was so ashamed that I went by her house because I thought I had caused her to have a heart attack. And I apologized to her. I asked her if she thought she needed to go to the hospital.

"She was saying, 'Oh, oh, God. Oh, me. I never thought I'd see that ugly face again,' and she was moaning," Beaver said. "I really thought she had had a heart attack."

Beaver testified that after her meeting with Fisher, she launched a second round of phone calls to the sheriff's office, and again received no call back.

"Who was the first person from a law enforcement standpoint that came to see you?" Johnson asked.

"That was Dale Bundy," Beaver said.

Johnson asked what it was that she had wanted to tell the original detectives all those years ago about Dennis Perry. "He told me that he asked the man for money, if he would loan him money to get back to Jonesboro and the man, Dennis said, 'put me down and made fun of me.'"

"What did he say he was going to do to that man?" Johnson asked.

"He said—he said—," she started.

A bomb was falling.

"He said, 'I always wondered what it was like to kill a n———, and now I'm going to get me one.'"

Johnson had no more questions.

Westling had many questions, mainly about why he hadn't heard so much of the information until just now, including that last bomb. It wasn't in Bundy's report, and Beaver had repeatedly declined to talk to the defense. Westling saw the glaring contradictions in Jane Beaver's story. In court she said that Perry told her he was going to kill Harold Swain several days before the murders, but she'd reported to Bundy that Perry told her his plan weeks before. Beaver said Perry had been living with his grandparents in the days before the murders, which wasn't true. She also offered a bizarre theory about how Perry walked home after the murders using hidden paths in the woods to avoid detection from police swarming Spring Bluff. Despite the discrepancies, the prosecution thought their star witness was doing great and holding up well to the defense's scrutiny.

After the testimony ended for the day, a deputy led Perry out of the courtroom, and that night, like the last eleven hundred, he went to sleep in jail.

ON THE WITNESS STAND THE NEXT DAY, DALE BUNDY HAD NEW stories too. The most critical was about Perry's "confession." Bundy described how Perry said many damaging things in the interrogation, including that he could've ridden a motorcycle to Camden County that weekend with his brother, but he couldn't remember. Bundy also said that during the back-and-forth, he stepped out of the interrogation room to get a drink of water, when an officer appeared, saying, "You need to get back here." Perry just confessed to being at the church, said the officer.

Bundy raced back to Perry, who again confessed that he was at the church. Bundy recalled speaking to Perry and how he led him right where he wanted him: "'Dennis, you've been afraid that this day was going to come for a long time, haven't you?' And he said, 'Yes.' I said, 'How long have you been worrying about this day coming?' His statement was, 'Since the first time you rolled into my driveway.'"

At the defense table, Perry felt disgusted and powerless. If he had his way, he would've jumped up and called Bundy a liar in front of everyone. But he could only listen and root for his attorney.

Westling used a key piece of evidence to discredit the detective. He got Bundy to admit that he hadn't paid attention to where the women were sitting in the church. He hadn't looked at the crime scene diagrams long enough to notice that a door blocked Cora Fisher's view of the killer. Fisher—who said in her testimony that she recognized the murderer, whose emotional reaction to the picture of Perry was at the heart of Beaver's story—evidently couldn't have seen the killer. Kennedy and Gregory had certainly noticed this, which was why they focused on other witnesses; they feared that Fisher was confused in all the trauma and that she wanted to be involved in the investigation. When Westling asked why Bundy hadn't noticed the diagram in five years of investigation, the detective had no answer.

This should've been a big moment in court, the kind of moment that forced the judge to stop the proceedings and reevaluate the evidence. Bundy's confession of ignorance on this major point could have been enough to drop the charges against Perry. But the judge didn't stop anything. She just listened.

Then Westling brought up a curious part of Bundy's investigative report: Beaver said Perry spoke about killing a man who sold drugs. The state hadn't said a word about that because there was no evidence that Harold Swain did any such thing.

"Did Deacon Swain deal drugs?" Westling asked Bundy.

"Not to my knowledge."

"He a drug dealer? A druggie?"

"No, sir."

Westling lingered on this point. He insisted that Perry had never told Beaver of any plans to kill anyone, but Westling needed to let the jury know that even if they believed the star witness's story, it was a story about Perry allegedly wanting to kill some drug dealer—not Harold Swain.

MONTHS BEFORE THE TRIAL, JOHNSON HAD GRANTED DONNIE Barrentine immunity from prosecution in the Swains' murders in exchange for his candid testimony. Westling asked the judge if he could enter the immunity document into evidence. There was a brief pause. Judge Amanda Williams, known as aggressive and prosecution-friendly, asked to see it herself. This was the first that she had heard of Barrentine receiving a grant of immunity.

But after brief deliberations, the judge approved the prosecutor's immunity decision and admitted the document into evidence.

Westling wanted the jury to study it. The wording ran against the state's theory of the case, saying that Barrentine *was present* at the scene but not the shooter: "DONNIE BARRENTINE was a witness to the death of Harold and Thelma Swain, was present at the scene and has given statements to other persons about his involvement. His testimony to such is necessary to the public interest. (The state) hereby grants to DONNIE BARRENTINE use and derivative use immunity in the trial of the case of the State of Georgia vs. Dennis Perry."

In court, Johnson did not argue—and never would—that Barrentine and Perry committed the murders together or that Barrentine was involved. The prosecutor did, however, have a long history of giving suspects immunity if they testified against other suspects. And he and so many other prosecutors had seen that juries would convict people even with holes in the story, that juries would fill in the blanks themselves if you gave them enough suspicion to work with.

When Barrentine took the stand, he denied any involvement in the murders at Rising Daughter Baptist and insisted that he wasn't at the scene—no matter what the immunity document said. Johnson all but dared Barrentine to confess to the murders, pointing out repeatedly that his immunity was absolute even if he told the court he killed the Swains. He could admit it and laugh in the jury's face. No matter what he said, he couldn't be charged.

Barrentine said he had nothing to confess.

Johnson told the jury he was thankful that Butch Kennedy and Joe Gregory were never able to charge Barrentine because, if that had happened, an innocent man might be in prison.

⁓

THE JURY BEGAN DELIBERATIONS AT 4 P.M. ON FEBRUARY 14.

In the hallway, Perry's supporters waited with the few local journalists. The family still felt confident. Some of the reporters were sure enough that Perry would be acquitted that they joked among themselves, wondering what was taking so long. The evidence seemed too convoluted and weak for conviction. The jury wasn't unanimous at first. But by 7:30 p.m., they'd reached a verdict.

Guilty on all counts.

Relatives of the Swains thanked God for justice. Perry felt like someone had reached into his chest and snatched out his soul. His whole body went weak.

Next was the penalty phase of the trial, in which the jury was to decide whether Perry should be executed by the state or sentenced to life. It was set to begin immediately, but John Johnson approached the defense. He had a new offer: If Perry would waive his rights to appeal, the state would agree to two life sentences instead of death.

Perry had only minutes to decide. He wasn't allowed to confer with his family.

His attorneys told him they suspected the jury would vote for death.

"Do you want to enter into this agreement with the state today?" Perry heard the judge ask.

He did not want to die. He wanted hope.

"Yes, ma'am," Perry said.

15

Caged

A corrections officer sent the men inside and ordered them to sit in barber chairs.

How would you like your hair cut? Perry was asked.

Leave a little on the sides, he said.

The man shaved his head. The illusion of choice. It was an old trick played on prisoners entering Middle Georgia's intake center. The men were sentenced to spend years, some of them all the years they had left, in prison—a horrible place to be in the best of conditions, and Georgia's prisons were terrible. They had a reputation for violence, crumbling health care services, and countless daily indignities. It was a life of deprivation, of having control over nothing—including your hair.

Perry was issued a white jumpsuit and an identification number, which, as far as the Georgia Department of Corrections was concerned, was his name. In the first two weeks, Perry learned that you didn't sleep in prison. The best you could do was nap. His bunk was surrounded by dozens of men, shifting and talking in bed, and the emergency lights stayed on all night. After quitting a few years earlier, Perry smoked cigarettes, largely so he could be outside in the sun for a few minutes. He tried to adjust to a life of being told what to do. If he wanted to step foot outside his dorm, make a call, or even visit Medical, he'd have to ask permission. He could only have visitors who were approved by the prison and at times the prison approved. He had no control, even, over which prison he was in.

Before long at Coastal State, a guard came to Perry in the middle of the night and told him to pack, he was moving. After a drowsy bus ride, he arrived at Autry State Prison, which was notorious for stabbings. Perry learned when he arrived that there'd just been a riot that started from a fight about undercooked chicken in the cafeteria.

He wondered how much worse things would get for him here. He kept to himself while he got used to the place. He wrote poems and drew, went to church in the prison chapel. He grieved over his divorce from Karen. Perry kept as busy as he could. He worked in the commissary, where he became close friends with his coworker, John, a tall Black man who happened to be Perry's bunkmate. Their personalities—Perry a people-loving extrovert, John a kind introvert—meshed, and they found they liked hearing stories about each other's family. Their connection was vital to surviving the brutality of prison. Neither asked the other about his conviction. Perry and John thanked God for one another.

SHORTLY AFTER THE TRIAL, KENNEDY WAS IN TOUCH WITH PERry's family. He asked some of them, including Perry's brother, to meet him in an out-of-the-way spot where no one would see them. Everyone in law enforcement had heard that Sheriff Smith had people all over Camden County who told him what they saw, and Kennedy didn't want any further problems with the sheriff. They met at night, in a car.

I know he's innocent, Kennedy said.

He told them to stay in touch, and this gave them the faintest hope. He said he would do what he could to help Perry, and even Kennedy had no idea what that could possibly be. Gregory also told the family he wanted to help.

Perry and his supporters could count a third officer who'd worked the case and believed in Perry's innocence in Mike Ellerson. But like the others, Ellerson, by then working for a local police department, had no idea how to help.

Even with shreds of hope from those three supporters, Perry's family grew more and more despondent. In his brother's second month in state prison, Daniel Perry didn't know what to do. So he wrote a letter on behalf of the family, sending it to Governor Sonny Perdue, various state lawmakers, and members of the media. He detailed the evidence—and poured his frustration onto the page: "Bill Smith is still the sheriff in this town. I guess you should be very careful if you happen to pass through Camden Co. Ga. especially if you look like someone he wants to target for one of his unsolved crimes, he must be reelected you see!" In the postscript, Daniel went for the reader's heart. "He has had to miss out on so many birthdays, anniversaries, baby births, weddings and such. Yet the rest of us go on, day in and out. Forgetting that it is a privilege to be FREE. Help us, set Dennis FREE."

He didn't receive a single reply.

IN THE EARLY 1980S, BRENDA HAHN TOOK NOTICE OF DENNIS Perry, who was about her age. He sold the fish door-to-door that he and his grandma had caught. Brenda's mother was a loyal customer. When Perry would stop by the house, Hahn found herself drawn to the kitchen window. From there, she could stare at him in the yard talking with her mom. He had the long stringy hair of country boys of the day and always seemed to be smiling. He had no idea she had a crush on him. Hahn recalled when she'd seen Perry at a backwoods bar, a place called Island Grove. Perry asked her for a ride to the store to buy cigarettes. She obliged, and to thank her, Perry gave her a friendly kiss on the cheek. Perry was single that night; Hahn had just been married. But she remembered that kiss.

Hahn, who ran the cafeteria at Camden County High School, knew Perry had gone to prison for murder, but she couldn't imagine he was guilty. In 2007, after her divorce and Perry's split with Karen, Hahn asked Perry's grandmother how she could reach him. She wrote him a letter. He wrote her back. After a few letters, Perry called, prepared with a good opening line:

Do you know who this is?

Who?

It's the rest of your life.

THE SAME YEAR, PERRY'S FAMILY GOT THE ATTENTION OF A journalist named Susan Greene at *The Denver Post*. Greene talked with many players in the case, including Perry. She interviewed him in prison, and Perry told her that the police had tried to coerce a confession from him.

"Dale Bundy started elaborating the story, with me saying 'I don't know.' He was trying to put words in my mouth," Perry said.

Joe Gregory told the reporter how he and Butch Kennedy had cleared Perry.

Asked why he'd written on the immunity document that "Barrentine was a witness to the death of Harold and Thelma Swain," Johnson told Greene that he didn't remember.

"At this point, I can't answer that question," he said.

Johnson also still couldn't account for the missing evidence, including the glasses that Gregory and Kennedy had found at the crime scene and believed belonged to the killer. To Perry, each piece of missing evidence represented one possible key to his release.

By this point, Perry was forty-five, and when he reflected on the case during his interview with Greene, he couldn't stop crying. "I can't believe I'm sitting here getting choked up about . . . glasses," he said. "But how do they lose evidence in a capital case? How do whole boxes of evidence slip through their fingers?"

～

BRENDA HAHN HAD STARTED MAKING THE TRIP FROM CAMDEN County to see Perry. It was more than three hours—a straight, boring shot to the west through fading towns of South Georgia. She passed the time thinking about Perry, wondering how their visit would go, how close the guards would let them sit. She made that drive each weekend. Visits piled up, and she was renting hotel rooms so she could extend her visits with Perry in the visitation area—a long, cinder block room with tables, vending machines, and one of those giant fundraiser thermometers on the wall—without having to drive home after dark.

Perry didn't like the idea of her driving at night. He was quickly falling for Hahn. He hadn't wanted to put his ex-wife through his incarceration, but here was Brenda knowing his plight going in, and she was OK with it. Perry took up wood carving and crafted intricate, artistic pieces. He sent them to Hahn, and she hung them on her walls at home so that, even though Perry wasn't with her, he surrounded her.

～

JULY 25, 2003. HIGHWAY 341, OUTSIDE BRUNSWICK, GEORGIA.

A police officer was stopped at a gas station after midnight when he saw a burgundy GMC Sonoma pickup truck pull onto the highway from an access road next to a convenience store—fast. The tires spun, and the truck fishtailed, prompting the cop to take off after it. The truck pulled over.

Erik Sparre, behind the driver's seat and smelling of alcohol, said he'd had a few beers and asked if he could call his parents to pick him up. The officer said no. Sparre was, according to the police report, unsteady in a field sobriety test and had a blood alcohol content of .175—double the legal limit.

After learning he was under arrest, Sparre began an hour-long tirade. It was far from his first arrest. In the early 1980s, he was accused of attacking a customer at Choo Choo BBQ. He'd been accused repeatedly of domestic violence. He was allegedly prolific with threats. He was accused of vowing to kill an ex's relative in 1990, of making other terroristic threats in 1995, threatening to burn down a house in 2000, threatening to shoot a neighbor and her dog in 2011. While threatening to kill his first ex-wife's family, he'd claimed he killed the Swains, leading to a terroristic threats charge.

Now, the officer took him to the jail for one more test on a breath analysis device. According to the police report, Sparre said, "I'm not taking no fucking test for you—you fucking pig, you can suck my dick, you fucking bitch."

At the emergency room, where, per protocol, Sparre had to be cleared for jail, he allegedly cursed out staff and spit all over the place.

"You are nothing but a n———-loving whore," Sparre told the officer, a man he'd seen around, "and I hope I see you leaving Pam's [a bar on Highway 17] because I'll make sure that you take a piss test, and you'll leave bloody."

The officer brushed off the threat and dropped Sparre off at jail.

16

Beginnings and Endings

In July 2007, three men boarded a small motorboat in St. Marys, headed for Cumberland Island. Leading the expedition was a firebrand local attorney named Jim Stein, a longtime critic of Sheriff Smith. He was taking a reporter and a photographer from Jacksonville's *Florida Times-Union* to see something that outraged him. At 10:30 a.m., the heat and humidity had already been at work for hours.

After forty-five minutes plodding down the East River, Stein docked the boat on the side of winding Old House Creek. Like everywhere else on Cumberland Island, it was lush—wild green with a thick canopy of pines and oaks. Insects swarmed the visitors. Stein noticed two boats already tied up, including one belonging to the sheriff's office. The attorney, reporter, and photographer walked up a road and started hearing what appeared to be construction noises. Stein smelled fresh-cut lumber. A sign read: "PRIVATE RESIDENCE BEYOND—NO ENTRY."

Just then they heard a vehicle coming and ducked into the woods until it passed. After they emerged, the journalists told Stein they couldn't go onto private property. Stein walked down the road alone. The trees cleared to reveal a private home, with two men building an addition onto it. One of them wore a blue uniform with a word on the back: "TRUSTEE." Stein asked what they were building. One man said it was going to be some sort of clinic. The journalists had their story: Sheriff Smith using prisoners as private laborers.

The construction was being done at the home of a doctor who was friends with the sheriff and who called his Cumberland Island house a "Confederate Embassy." Stein was outraged. The sight of a Black man working in bondage recalled the horrors of slavery that took place on this very island. The doctor evidently intended to treat Smith's son, Blake, a former Camden County deputy who was paralyzed in a car wreck. The sheriff would maintain that Blake wouldn't be the only patient, that the "center" would help plenty of people. The sheriff's office sent deputies to interview the reporter and photographer, who both declined to answer questions. They ran the story on the front page of that Sunday's paper.

SOON A TEAM OF GBI AGENTS WAS IN TOWN TO INVESTIGATE Sheriff Smith's use of prisoner labor again. As before, Smith called it "political," a "witch hunt." A parade of prisoners sat down for interviews, saying they worked on Cumberland Island and received no pay other than the $50 per week that trustees always got for helping around the jail.

Ronnie Moore, a fifty-two-year-old Black trustee, said he'd painted and picked up trash at the sheriff's friend's house.

"Were you paid?"

"I haven't been paid yet, but [the sheriff has] got a check for me," said Moore. "He told me that today."

"Is this the first time you knew that you were going to get paid—today?"

"Yes." Moore laughed awkwardly.

<center>~~~~~</center>

TOMMY GREGORY WOULD ADMIT THAT HE WAS AN ANGRY FORmer employee of Sheriff Smith's. He knew all about his dad's frustration with Smith from the Swain case and others. Tommy worked almost twenty years at the sheriff's office, watching how the boss operated. "The longer he was in, he got to where the law didn't apply to him. He *was* the law," Tommy once said. He'd been laid off in 2004 and, it appeared to Tommy, replaced by a friend of the sheriff's. Tommy took a job at the same police department as Mike Ellerson. And he stewed for four years until he decided to stand up to Smith.

Dad, Tommy told Joe Gregory on the phone, *I'm gonna run for sheriff.*

You know what kind of political machine Bill Smith has, Joe said. *He'll stop at nothing to beat you.*

Tommy said he thought enough people were angry and ready for change.

Smith's last challenger, retired Navy investigations officer and teacher Rich Gamble, had railed against the sheriff's misuse of seized drug money. Tommy Gregory picked up the torch, making the issue a centerpiece of his campaign. Tommy amped up his rhetoric as more newspaper exposés appeared. All the buzz prompted the GBI team to start investigating the sheriff's use of drug money in addition to prisoner labor. The agents got an email each time a new article was published. It was hard to keep up. Smith had used drug money to buy uniforms for local high school cheerleaders. He'd donated to the

Citadel—a college that wasn't even in Georgia but was his alma mater. He'd donated to the Shepherd Center in Atlanta after his son was treated there. He'd bought schoolbooks for friends' children.

An even more striking item appeared in a 2003 statement from the sheriff's seized asset account: a $12,000 payment to Jane Beaver. Next to her name it said: "REWARD." It's illegal to provide a reward to a witness without disclosing it. It was a huge discovery, the kind that could lead to further scrutiny on Perry's case and could cause his conviction to be tossed.

The trouble was, none of the agents who saw this record had worked on the Swain case. They had no idea who Jane Beaver was or why it would be significant for her to have received a reward. If anything, a reward for information about a crime seemed to be one potentially legal use of seized drug money.

And so, this document that could've saved Perry was of no help to him. At least not yet.

FOR THE FIRST TIME IN TWO DECADES, THE RACE FOR SHERIFF seemed competitive. Smith was seventy, silver hair still thick, and game to defend himself against the mounting allegations. But it was getting harder. A member of the Camden County Board of Commissioners went to the GBI to report that Sheriff Smith was submitting deputies to voice stress analysis—something like a modern and still dubious polygraph—to find out who was talking to the GBI. Commissioners railed against the sheriff, saying that he was giving the county a bad name. They threatened to take control of the confiscated money, to seize Smith's biggest asset.

By the time of the preelection debate on June 6, 2008, Smith knew he couldn't deny the allegations anymore. The event was held at the St.

Marys chapter of the Fraternal Order of Eagles, which sat next door to the St. Marys Police Department. The sheriff's race led the event, and Sheriff Smith appeared determined to take control of the narrative by . . . mostly confirming it.

Yes, Smith confessed, he'd taken a prisoner to South Carolina. Yes, he'd had that man build a handicap shower and wheelchair ramp for his son in his ex-wife's house. Yes, Smith said, he had subjected deputies to stress tests after they'd spoken with the GBI. But he'd served the community for decades and they could count on him to put Camden County first.

Tommy Gregory let the crowd know that regardless of his "confession," Smith didn't truly intend to be accountable to the voters.

"I believe in an open, honest government," Gregory said. And what else did he need to say? This election was Sheriff Smith versus Not Sheriff Smith.

The sheriff's sudden candor didn't do much for him. People were angry. He even had a bruising appearance on NPR's *All Things Considered*, whose journalists pressed him on the drug money controversy. "I'd say Camden County has probably been one of the most successful agencies on the Eastern seaboard in seizing money belonging to the drug dealers," Smith told a reporter, sitting in his office.

Steve Berry, a county commissioner, lawyer, and novelist, told NPR how Smith had prisoners working on his getaway house. "The Ponderosa probably represents the pinnacle of abuse," Berry said. "The sheriff buys a piece of property in the center of the county, little old house on it, takes inmates out there, they rebuild the entire house into a very nice party house."

"That's completely untrue," said the sheriff. "Must be a figment of his imagination. I think you probably know he's a fiction writer, and he's pretty good with that." The story aired across the country with the election just weeks away.

～

HISTORY ARRIVED ON THE BACKS OF A FEW HUNDRED VOTERS.

On July 18, 2008, Sheriff Bill Smith's twenty-two-year reign and the family dynasty at the sheriff's office ended. Voters chose Tommy Gregory.

Joe Gregory and Butch Kennedy were amazed to see the giant fall, and they were proud of Tommy for being the one to make it happen. They predicted, correctly, that Smith wouldn't be charged in the latest GBI investigation, but his power was hobbled. Dennis Perry felt satisfaction at learning of Sheriff Smith's defeat, but what could it really mean for him? The filings, hearings, and petitions to challenge his conviction were going nowhere. Ironically, if the prosecutor had given Perry the death penalty, he would've been entitled to a post-conviction attorney. But as it now stood, the state of Georgia had no legal obligation to provide him with one—and thus didn't.

Still, it brought comfort to know that a few officers, and maybe even the new sheriff, were on his side. Perry also had strong supporters in his family, his bunkmate John, and Brenda Hahn. Perry and Hahn were married in January 2009 at Autry State Prison. Perry's mother and grandmother were allowed to attend the small ceremony in the chapel. To celebrate their union, prison officials gave the couple an extra twenty or thirty minutes to visit. All the same rules about touch applied: they could hug and kiss, but only for a few seconds before the guards broke them apart.

They felt closer, married, though 160 miles still separated them. Sometimes Brenda Perry would get so caught up in imagining the life they could have together that she'd feel Dennis there with her. She'd feel his hand on her leg while she was driving, and for a moment she could swear he was in the passenger's seat. Brenda started taking her friend Michelle with her to the prison. Soon, Michelle and Perry's bunkmate John fell in love and were married, too.

Because Perry's case was subject to state laws as they were at the time of the double murder in 1985, he was eligible for parole after fourteen years. But you had pretty much no chance at parole if you refused to admit to the crime and express remorse. John had been convicted of murder, too. But John had admitted it and felt remorse, which he expressed to parole officials. One day in 2010, John was sent to a halfway house in Atlanta—a sign that he would soon be granted parole. Meantime, he would be assigned to work at the governor's mansion, where he would become close with Governor Nathan Deal and First Lady Sandra Deal. News of John's move thrilled Perry, but it also meant they might never see each other again. John would be on parole for the rest of his life and unable to visit the prison, and Perry didn't know how he'd ever get out.

NOT LONG AFTER JOHN LEFT, PERRY WAS LISTENING TO HIS radio when, in his peripheral vision, he saw a man coming toward him with a sharp metal rod. As Perry turned around, the man stabbed him in the back.

Perry kicked the attacker in the face, fighting for his life against the attacker and his friends. Outmatched, Perry broke free and retreated out of the dorm, into the dayroom. He found a guard.

I just got stabbed!

It turned out the man wanted to steal a flip phone from Perry. Instead of just demanding the phone, the man stabbed Perry without warning. After the fight, Perry was sent to the hole, bandaged up. Why? He wasn't supposed to have a cell phone.

The wound would soon heal, but Perry's body and spirits were flagging. Brenda and Dennis worried what was next for him. They took solace in knowing that the Georgia Innocence Project seemed to believe in Perry's wrongful conviction, but the nonprofit didn't have the resources to commit to a reinvestigation of the murders at Rising Daughter. That's what the attorneys thought it would take to figure out how to untangle the bizarre knot of evidence and testimony that led to Perry's conviction.

Dennis prayed, asking God to send people to help him. He told Brenda he was going to pray his way to freedom.

17

Undisclosed

In 2018, Susan Simpson, one of the attorneys who hosted the *Undisclosed* podcast, heard about Dennis Perry's conviction. The show examined potential wrongful conviction cases and was started by Rabia Chaudry, the attorney for Adnan Syed, whose murder conviction was examined by the groundbreaking podcast *Serial*. Simpson, a metro Atlanta native, was asked to investigate Perry's case by the Georgia Innocence Project. *Undisclosed* had already done a season about another of the nonprofit's clients and uncovered new evidence that would eventually lead to an innocent man's freedom. Simpson was known as a relentless investigator, but even she felt daunted by the Swain case. The police investigation had been sprawling and unorthodox, not to mention the fact that it had been thirty-three years since the murders. Then she called Butch Kennedy, and he encouraged her to investigate. Kennedy, retired from the tax commissioner's office, was thinking even more about his failure to solve the Swain murders lately, fantasizing about getting his hands on the case file one more time to try to get to the truth. He knew that was just a dream. But Simpson?

Kennedy tried not to get his hopes up, but this woman seemed like she could get things done.

Simpson had a good sense of humor and was the type of person who gets labeled a "force of nature." That's because she was so dogged and probing that when she got on a case, it could feel like a hurricane was coming through to sweep away all the lies and misconceptions. Simpson, as usual, started her investigation into the Swains' murders by collecting as many documents as she could. Thousands of pages of records from the sheriff's office, the GBI, and the DA's office filled several banker's boxes. In total, there were six thousand pages. Simpson moved into a house in Woodbine with a list of people to interview all over the county. First she wanted to talk with Bundy, but she worried that he'd decline an interview. When Simpson showed up at the sheriff's office in July 2018 to interview him, Bundy was friendly and said he wanted to tell the story. He said there was no doubt Perry was guilty. Bundy said he would stand by his work.

Bundy said that the case file was a wreck when he found it. A lot of evidence was missing, including the glasses that the original detectives thought belonged to the killer. "There was a lot of stuff that went missing, got disorganized," Bundy said. "If those glasses were in the file, I don't know. The only evidence I ever saw from that case . . . were the shirt buttons, a pair of glasses that had been identified as belonging to Harold Swain, and some wire clippings." Bundy wasn't concerned about the missing glasses because Perry didn't wear glasses, and Bundy called them irrelevant. As for missing documents, Bundy said they might've gone missing when the GBI was investigating Sheriff Bill Smith in the early 1990s. But he insisted that Joe Gregory was wrong about Perry's alibi. There wasn't a record of Gregory contacting Perry's boss because he never did, Bundy said, suggesting that the old GBI agent had mixed Perry up with some other forgotten suspect.

"I've been drug through the wringer on this case," Bundy said. "I've been made to look like just a horrible person that framed this poor innocent man. And I know I put a lot of my time in this case, I was very careful with it. The last thing I'd want to do is to put someone in prison that I didn't think was guilty."

He said that Kennedy and Gregory never identified Perry as the killer because of their focus on Donnie Barrentine. "They got tunnel vision," Bundy said. Simpson was well aware of that phenomenon. Simpson had seen a pattern of "tunnel vision" in the wrongful conviction cases she'd investigated. She knew that she, too, had to keep an open mind and just follow the evidence. Simpson was open to any possibility, including that Perry was guilty. But as she listened to Bundy talk, Simpson wondered how clear his vision was on the biggest case of his career.

SCROLLING THROUGH THE CASE FILE, SIMPSON FOUND A SUR-prising memo: a message Jane Beaver left for prosecutor John Johnson dated January 14, 2000, the day after Perry's arrest. Written in shorthand, the memo said that Beaver had a question about reward money: "[She] says it was because of the picture & info she turned in that case solved. Said she tried to give the sheriff info several times over the years & they wouldn't listen. Says they have told her that the reward $ is no longer there. Please call her. She wants to collect reward."

This was striking to Simpson. If Beaver received a reward without the state disclosing that to the defense, it could be ruled a constitutional violation. There was no record in the case file of Beaver receiving a reward. Simpson wanted to ask Beaver about it, but she couldn't be interviewed. She was in a nearby nursing home and had been diagnosed with dementia about five years after the trial. She died on September 19, 2018, soon after the *Undisclosed* investigation began.

Simpson was also looking into Donnie Barrentine but found herself vexed by missing evidence. She couldn't find a report from the 1985 interview with Barrentine by the outside interrogator, Dixie Glenn Foster. That interview had been damning enough that it led Kennedy to compose a warrant for Barrentine's arrest. There was evidence that detectives had access to Foster's report in 2002, less than a year before Perry's trial, but it had since vanished.

Simpson tracked down Foster, who had moved to Australia. He was surprised to hear there was no report in the file. During the interrogation, Foster said, Barrentine confessed to the murders. Foster said Barrentine made statements that showed he was either the killer or present at the scene with the killer. Barrentine had described how the murder weapon was discarded into a body of water. Foster said he sent his report directly to then-DA Glenn Thomas, who died a decade before Simpson came to town. After learning that Thomas was shutting down the investigation into Barrentine, Foster had contacted the Georgia Attorney General's Office, as well as the US Department of Justice, and asked that they look into Thomas's handling of the case. Foster never heard back from either.

This was an enormous finding. The state hadn't turned over a copy of Foster's report to the defense. A failure like this by the state could be grounds to overturn a conviction.

STILL TRACING THE LEAD ABOUT JANE BEAVER'S REWARD, SIMPSON went to see Beaver's daughter, Carol Anne Raborn, who'd dated Perry in the mid-1980s. Raborn lived in a mobile home down a dirt road in Camden County.

Raborn admitted she doubted Perry's guilt. Her mother's troubles with the truth and reality were well known. Raborn remembered a time when Beaver overreacted in the extreme to a comment Perry made during a visit. Jokingly, he said he could kill someone—not Harold Swain—over some small transgression. It'd just been a joke. But Beaver started screaming and ordered Perry out of her house. "She told me to get him out of here—actually, get him the hell out of here, she said to us," Raborn said. "So, we got in the car and left."

Simpson asked if her mother had gotten a reward. Raborn said her mother was at least aware of the reward. "Mama told me about it. She said she'd seen it on (a) crime program."

But did Beaver receive it? Raborn said she didn't know.

Undisclosed started releasing episodes about the case, and prison staff allowed Perry to listen to each one in a drab office. Perry sat rapt as Simpson described interviewing Donnie Barrentine at his home. She also highlighted how Mike Ellerson had gotten frozen out of Bundy's investigation. "I came to my conclusion that he didn't do it, [and] I was off. I was gone," Ellerson told Simpson. "I had nothing else to do with that case."

While listening to these episodes, Perry had to pause often, overwhelmed by grief or fury. He hoped that a lot of people were listening and that this would shake something loose. Even more, Perry hoped Simpson could find something to solve the case and prove who really killed the Swains. He was angry that the killer never paid for what he'd done. Perry couldn't be interviewed on the podcast because the Georgia Department of Corrections didn't allow prisoners to speak to the press—unless it was a sunny story about some rehabilitation program officials wanted to promote.

One day, Perry heard Simpson close the loop on the reward money question. She was reading a muckraking anonymous local blog when she happened upon evidence. On the site were bank records from the sheriff's office—Sheriff Smith's drug money fund. One of the line items was a payment of $12,000 to Jane Beaver. Next to her name it said: "REWARD." A payment in the same amount had been made to Corky Rozier, the man who called *Unsolved Mysteries* about Perry killing Harold Swain to keep him quiet about a field of marijuana. Rozier was a friend of Sheriff Smith's, but he never testified, and his false story wasn't even used in the facts presented to the jury to convict Perry. The outrage Perry felt would echo for months. It haunted him that Jane Beaver, someone he'd known for years and never said a cross word to, was the star witness against him. He knew how damaged she had been by trauma, but it was devastating to think that her motive to send him away on a lie was money. At the same time, Perry was anxious and even excited to hear what Simpson would uncover next.

ACCOMPANIED BY AN INTERN, SIMPSON KNOCKED ON THE DOOR of one of the last living church witnesses, Gwen Owens, one of the four women who said they saw the killer's face and contributed to the composite sketch. The other three women, Vanzola Williams, Lettie Frazier, and Cora Fisher, had died. Bundy had interviewed Owens, but his report made no mention of it, and speaking with *Undisclosed*, he brushed aside Owens and her daughter Leslie, who'd been only seven at the time of the murders, as uncooperative.

"I was actually talking to Dale Bundy," Simpson told Owens, "and he told me that he thought that y'all had always known who the killer was but were too afraid to tell them back then."

"That's a lie," Owens said, emphatically.

Simpson asked her to look at the composite sketch from 1985. Simpson asked if it looked like the man who killed the Swains. Owens studied it for a few seconds.

"No. It doesn't," Owens said, echoing what she'd told the police back then.

They started talking about Cora Fisher's identification and Vanzola Williams's partial identification when Owens interjected with a bit of caution, saying that not everything the other witnesses had said was necessarily true: "Some of the ladies might exaggerate," Owens said. Not all, Owens was quick to reiterate, but some.

Around the time she spoke with Owens, Simpson found there had been another woman at Rising Daughter when the murders happened. Her name never made it on the list of witnesses, but she was one of the women who could have seen the killer. Afraid of revealing her name publicly, the new witness asked Simpson to refer to her only by the pseudonym Lavinia. Lavinia said she never spoke with Kennedy, Gregory, or Bundy. But she had talked with a Woodbine police officer who had been the first to the scene.

It was a chaotic scene after the murders, with police trying to figure out who had been inside during the shooting while some witnesses, shaken beyond belief, went straight home to be with their families. The records of Lavinia's witness statement never made it to the sheriff's office. Lavinia's story from that night appeared credible, and she had doubts about whether the police got the right man. As much as she cared for Cora Fisher, Lavinia said she thought that Fisher was wrong about Perry—she thought the real killer was still out there. That's why Lavinia didn't want to reveal her name.

"She was a little bit flighty," Lavinia said of Fisher. "I didn't want to say that, because that's not nice to say."

⁓

CLEARLY, GREGORY AND KENNEDY HADN'T KNOWN ABOUT Lavinia and neither had Bundy. Simpson couldn't much blame Bundy for missing the witness, especially when the on-scene detectives missed her. But as Simpson dug deeper, there was something about Bundy's investigation, particularly the early days when he was speaking with witnesses from the church, that gave her pause. This had been one of the most confounding cases in local memory, yet the newly hired cold case cop identified Perry as the killer on the seventh day of his investigation in 1998. He was told that Perry was the killer by the first witness he interviewed, Cora Fisher, a curious choice. Why choose Cora Fisher first instead of Vanzola Williams? Williams saw the gunman up close, and her story had always aligned with the other witness statements, while Fisher's hadn't. Why hadn't he considered Barrentine as a serious suspect?

Simpson was pressing Bundy on this on the phone one day, to confirm the timeline of his investigation when he became angry. He'd already sat for more than two hours with Simpson to answer questions. He'd taken follow-up calls. He knew Simpson feared he'd sent an innocent man to prison. He started shouting through the phone.

Take your fucking investigation, Bundy said, *and shove it up your fucking ass.*

PART III

THE TIDE COMES BACK

Summer brings hurricanes that make the tide mean. When a storm is kicking up, the alligators and birds in the marshes flee for a safe place to wait it out. The force of the waves, coupled with the driving wind, rip up reeds and spit them onto land. When the tide breaches the banks, waves carry fiddler crabs and small fish into homes, where salt water rises over residents' ankles. Unlike wildlife, many people don't heed the warnings of danger to come. They ignore even mandatory evacuations, reasoning that Coastal Georgia never sees a powerful hit, and resolve to stand up to the storm, to think that they'll be spared, as they always have been, to think that nothing ever really changes here.

18

Through the Glass Door

In downtown Waycross, Georgia, my hometown, a stone soldier stands several stories aloft on a marble pedestal, outfitted with a rifle and a wide-brimmed hat. On the base of the monument, the words of Confederate president Jefferson Davis are inscribed: "The impartial enlightened verdict of mankind will vindicate the rectitude of our conduct, and he who knows the hearts of men, will judge the sincerity with which we labored to preserve the government of our fathers in its spirit."

A few paces from the monument, as a kid I sat on top of an accompanying cannon, smiling, asking my mom to take my picture on her disposable camera. As an eight-year-old white child, I didn't know a thing about the monument in the heart of my hometown. Later I would learn the facts: the Waycross Confederate Monument stands in a city that did not exist—was just pines and swamp—until twenty-five years after the Civil War. The memorial to Confederate dead, whose inscription honors the fight to preserve slavery, was installed in 1910, in the segregation era. While Black Georgians pressed for basic rights, white residents erected a monument of a Confederate soldier, rifle ready, with a cannon at his feet and a quote from Jefferson Davis. The statue sent a message to Black people through the ages: This is our place, not yours. And because South Georgia is a place rife with cognitive dissonance, I've seen Black children pose for the same picture, as oblivious as I was. The African American pastor who would become the second Black mayor of Waycross after 2019 worked in an office just six hundred feet from the Confederate monument.

This was the world I grew up in—a forty-five-minute drive from Rising Daughter Baptist Church. In the early 1990s, around the time of the photo of me on the cannon, the two local school districts were combined to integrate the schools. I attended an elementary school with a few hundred kids, and no more than a handful were Black, even though more than a third of the county was African American. My father was the longtime athletic trainer at the majority-Black high school. After the districts were combined, I moved to a school that was about half Black, and my dad went to the new Ware County High, which was created by the merger of the majority-Black high school and the majority-white one. While more local Black kids and white kids spent time together at school, groups still formed on racial lines, and in the early 2000s, when I was in high school, interracial dating remained rare. The few kids who dared cross that line were ostracized.

This is why, when the Georgia Innocence Project approached me in August 2019 about the murders at Rising Daughter Baptist, I was interested to learn that a purported white supremacist had been a suspect. My job was covering crime and public safety for *The Atlanta Journal-Constitution*, Georgia's largest paper. I'd covered hundreds of homicide cases. I'd sat in courtrooms and watched numerous murder trials and seen almost every single person get convicted. Leaders at the Georgia Innocence Project thought Perry's case could benefit from a story in the *AJC*, which had a reputation for large investigations that

changed laws for the better and sent corrupt officials tumbling out
of office, sometimes into prison. Months earlier, in January 2019, my
reporting on the murders of two children found buried in their family's backyard led to changes in state child welfare policy and a new
law intended to better protect vulnerable children. I'd already seen
how hard truths could change Georgia for the better. I was also coming off a case involving three men wrongfully convicted of murder in
Savannah, where an eyewitness tried to help me identify the real killer.
I never got there, but I still got closer to solving the case than I even
imagined. That experience gave me—someone who'd spent most of
his life without much confidence—the audacity to think that maybe I
could build on what others had uncovered before me and finally solve
the Swain case.

At the urging of the Georgia Innocence Project, I listened to
the *Undisclosed* season about the Swains' murders. It was an impressive twenty-four hours long and full of huge findings about corruption and leads. In Simpson's reporting, I first encountered the people
who'd loom so large in my mind over the next months and years. I
learned about Harold and Thelma Swain, who reminded me of my
grandparents, also deeply religious and raised on family farms and at
cherished rural churches. Having spent a lifetime in South Georgia—
encountering screaming rebel flag–wavers like Erik Sparre, fishing the
same rivers as Harold Swain and Dennis Perry, and driving the same
highways as Butch Kennedy and Dale Bundy—I felt powerfully drawn
to the story.

I had worried I wouldn't be able to add much after *Undisclosed* had
devoted an entire season to the case. The podcast proved how weak the
case against Perry was, that the state had hidden evidence from the
defense. Simpson, one of the most determined and discerning investigators I'd ever met, found enough for a blistering habeas corpus filing

by Perry's lawyers. It was pending with no court date set. Still, I had unanswered questions. I was surprised that Kennedy and Gregory's favorite suspect was ex–drug trafficker Donnie Barrentine, given that Erik Sparre, a purported white supremacist, had allegedly told two ex-wives that he'd killed the Swains. As a native of the area, I asked myself what seemed most likely: Did a drug gang kill two innocent people in a church—and leave more than a few witnesses—to get back at their drug-trafficking relative? Or did a racist who had some issue with Harold Swain shoot them down and get away with it? Simpson encouraged me to investigate. It turned out she'd wanted to investigate Erik Sparre further but had run out of time before *Undisclosed* had to turn to its next case.

ALL THE SAME, IT WAS RARE FOR ANY NEWSPAPER, EVEN A LEAD-ing one like the *AJC*, to allow a reporter to take on an innocence investigation, especially one more than two hundred miles outside of metro Atlanta. The *AJC* had been gutted in the past decade—cut down from 500 employees to 150. Some of the paper's best and most dedicated journalists were scrambling for work or had left the indus-try entirely. The number of seasoned editors had been slashed, and as a result, there were fewer of the riveting investigations that the paper was known for. Generally, my editors wouldn't have considered let-ting me dedicate myself to one story. But they needed big projects to uphold the paper's tradition of investigative journalism and rich sto-rytelling. So, I was given the über rare privilege to tune out the news and dig into one project.

I had to look at the whole case, all three suspects—Perry, Bar-rentine, and Sparre—and any others who might turn up. I had to learn the evidence, including what *Undisclosed* had amassed, and develop it further. Any possibility was on the table. I had to drive sandy backroads, knock on doors, make cold calls, sift through musty papers in the backs of courthouses, and, sources kept telling me, watch my back.

Even with the missing documents, the six-thousand-page case file left me with numerous questions and dozens of people to find. The podcast provided me with a road map, which helped focus my reporting by allowing me to avoid tripping down rabbit holes that didn't seem to go anywhere. I knew from the podcast that Dale Bundy, the detective who started the case against Perry, might be up for talking. I decided to start my interviews with him.

AFTER CHECKING INTO A DECAYING COMFORT SUITES IN LATE August 2019, I drove to the Camden County Sheriff's Office. Waves of heat rose from the parking lot pavement as I walked toward Dale Bundy's office. I hadn't called ahead. I preferred to just knock when visiting officials who might have reservations about an interview.

After I knocked, Bundy promptly appeared on the doorstep—the big man with a military buzz cut. I told him I was a reporter with *The Atlanta Journal-Constitution* who had questions about a case. His face turned sour. He looked like he was preparing to be punched in the face or getting ready to throw one.

Which case? Bundy asked.

The Dennis Perry case.

Fuck that, he said emphatically. Bundy said that his name had been tarnished unfairly by the Georgia Innocence Project and the podcast.

The man was guilty as sin, Bundy said, turning his back on me. He stepped back into his office, closed the door, and turned the lock.

For a moment, I stood mystified. I hadn't even asked a question yet. As a reporter, I decided years ago to forgive a slammed door or hung-up phone. Sometimes it takes a person a minute to warm to the idea of talking. A few moments later, I approached the door again.

What do you want? he said through the muffling door.

I think we got off on the wrong foot!

He swung open the door, stepped past me, and stomped toward the main sheriff's office building.

I called out: *Sir, I haven't done anything to you!*

He turned back and hollered: *And you won't neither!*

When Bundy made it inside the building, I would later learn, he put in notice that he was retiring.

THE SAME DAY, I WENT TO SEE CYNTHIA CLAYTON. CAMDEN County, and particularly Spring Bluff, was still the kind of place where something you said can beat you across town, and I wanted to be the one to inform the Swains' beloved niece of what I was doing and why. Clayton had acted as the informal spokesperson for the family for many years because they had so few close relatives left in the area.

Clayton invited me inside her Spring Bluff home. We sat in the living room of the ranch-style house while her mother, Thelma's Swain's little sister, watched television in another room. On the coffee table in front of Clayton was her Bible. It seemed likely to me that she wasn't entirely comfortable with all the renewed attention on the murders. Clayton was exceedingly kind to me, but I knew from *Undisclosed* that she believed that Perry did it and that his conviction had brought her relief after nearly twenty years of heartache. It felt important to explain myself.

"I've seen a copy of the most recent appeal that Dennis Perry filed," I said. "I've covered a lot of homicide cases, probably several hundred at this point, and there's some surprising things in there." I told her that I was afraid mistakes had been made and that Perry might be innocent, that the real killer might still be out there. I told her I desperately didn't want the Swains to be forgotten either, explaining that I wanted to represent them as the real, beloved people they were in anything I wrote.

"I guess Dennis Perry has the right to do what he's doing," Clayton said. "My belief is what happened in the courtroom and what the jury heard."

Clayton did not hate Dennis Perry. She was just glad that he saw justice. Her family and church witnesses never wanted Perry to receive the death penalty. They told prosecutor John Johnson that they opposed capital punishment because of their faith. "They were believers," Cynthia told me, referring to her aunt and uncle. "We're believers, and the hope is that we will see each other again. Things happen in life, and you deal with it the best as you can. Yes, I do want justice to be served and him to be held accountable. But killing him was not going to change the circumstances of what happened."

I wondered: Did John Johnson ever really intend to seek a death sentence, or was it just leverage to scare Perry? That pressure led him to waive his appeal rights in a deal with the state to avoid death. But I didn't bring this up with Clayton.

I wanted to ask her what she thought of what I was doing.

She said she didn't have a problem with what I was doing, though she pointed out that after Simpson, I was the second person to come around suddenly in the last year, bringing up awful memories and going after her comfort. Here I was wondering if the killer got away with it and was still out there free—a fear she thought she overcame nineteen years earlier with Perry's arrest.

"It's not fun," Clayton said.

She did still have her own questions about the case, though. Clayton had always wondered about Donnie Barrentine and if he fit in with Perry somehow.

Clayton agreed that her aunt and uncle—and what they meant to loved ones—should be represented in my coverage. In service of that, she was generous with her memories. She had always tried to spend more time with her good ones than her bad ones. She savored her memories of Uncle Harold complimenting her cooking, helping neighbors, and sitting in the den reading his Bible under the lamplight before bed. She remembered Aunt Thelma teaching her to make cornbread, watching *Guiding Light*, and making a quilt for her to take off to college.

Clayton stood up and walked into another room, returning with the quilt. Smiling, she unfurled it to display the patches of teal and yellow and green intersecting with bright multicolor stripes.

Just then, her mother, Earnestine Clayton, walked in. She was ninety-two and slight. She smiled, telling me about playing in the yard with her sister Thelma in the 1930s. They both loved softball and went to each other's games to cheer. The girls helped out on their stepfather's farm, planting sweet potatoes and shelling peas from the time they were small.

Earnestine remembered the night of the murders thirty-four years later. She worked at the hotel portion of the Cloister at Sea Island, the opulent and breathtakingly expensive resort, and had gotten off work but was waiting for her husband to finish his shift at Hercules, the rosin factory on the coast. Then the phone rang. It was Cynthia with unbelievable news. Earnestine went quiet and looked down. She had never stopped missing Thelma.

MY INVESTIGATION INTO ERIK SPARRE STARTED WITH A BREAK-
through. The first person I called to ask about him said that Sparre told
them he killed the Swains. This source had never spoken to investigators or a reporter about this. But they gave details that made the story
seem credible. Then, as with some other sources I would encounter,
this person asked me to promise never to reveal their identity. They
said they didn't know what Sparre would do if he found out what
they told me.

It was a strong lead, but I'd need to interview everyone I could
before committing to one story. Because twenty years had passed
since Perry was arrested and thirty-four since the murders, there were
many people I couldn't speak with. Cora Fisher, Vanzola Williams,
and Lavinia, the overlooked church witness Simpson had found, were
gone. Jane Beaver was gone, too.

Butch Kennedy remained. We met at a park on the Satilla River.
We sat on opposite sides of a picnic table under a covered pavilion as
bugs screeched, and our voices echoed in the tin roof. He'd put me
off a few days before meeting to talk about the case and looked like
he was about to cry when he explained it was because his dog had
died. His shame was what struck me most. He was soft-spoken and
repentant, telling me with his raspy tenor how he'd failed Harold and
Thelma Swain, the witnesses, the church, the Spring Bluff community, and Dennis Perry. He seemed like one of the most haunted men
I'd ever met.

I asked if he remembered a man named Erik Sparre. He did. He
recalled a "hellion" who he thought looked like the composite sketch
of the killer. Sparre lived in Spring Bluff, so he would've known Harold
Swain like everyone else, Kennedy said. He remembered when Emily
Head, Sparre's ex-wife, called the sheriff's office to say that Sparre had

beaten her up and was headed to the convenience store where Harold Swain worked. Kennedy said Sparre ignored him when told he was under arrest, starting to drive away. Kennedy had to reach inside, pull Sparre out, and take him to jail. Kennedy also remembered the time at the Choo Choo BBQ order window when Sparre allegedly attacked a brown-skinned man before trying to break his car windshield.

The more he thought about it, the more Kennedy liked the idea of Sparre as a suspect. He felt hope rising in him—unfamiliar after all those years. Perhaps Sparre, the old detective thought, fit into the case somehow with Donnie Barrentine, who Kennedy had long believed was guilty. But what about Sparre's alibi, that he'd been working the night of the murders? Kennedy said alibis could be false.

19

"If I Had Confessed to That"

It was September 2019, burning up hot with cottony clouds over the tree line. I'd come to the outskirts of the outskirts of Marianna, Florida, unannounced. I didn't know if Donnie Barrentine would be home, but I didn't want to call him. I needed to look him in the eye when we spoke. As I drove up a rough dirt road, a gaggle of chickens squawked in Barrentine's front yard. I walked to the front door of the mobile home and found a sign announcing: "WOOF: SEVERAL SPOILED DOGS LIVE HERE." I could hear the dogs barking and the sounds of some true crime TV show. I knocked and Barrentine opened the door. He was sixty-three, wiry and restless, with a thick mustache that made him look like Burt Reynolds's hard-living cousin. I introduced myself as a reporter from South Georgia looking into a case that I wanted to ask him about. This was the thing I said that made Dale Bundy look like he wanted to punch me. But Barrentine was immediately welcoming.

Which case? he asked, grinning. It had been only months since *Undisclosed* investigated him.

Come on, man, I laughed, *You know which case.*

He smiled and said it must be the church murders. He invited me
to his porch to talk things through.

I had two key questions for Barrentine. The first one was whether
he confessed to Dixie Glenn Foster in 1985, like Foster claimed to
Undisclosed. Barrentine didn't have to think long before answering.

"If I had confessed to that," he said flatly, rocking in a weather-
beaten chair, "I wouldn't be sitting here." Also, he said, he was an athe-
ist, but even he wouldn't kill someone in a church. And he certainly
wouldn't be foolish enough to leave so many witnesses. The idea was
an insult to his intelligence.

I asked Barrentine about the original investigation back in the
1980s and how he'd felt about being a suspect. He said the cops were
hell-bent—and wrong about him. He thought he was going to be
charged. That experience was one reason why he sometimes thought
the world would be better if they emptied all the prisons and filled
them back up with lawmen. Cops don't care if they have the right man,
he said—they just want someone in prison. As we spoke, side by side in
rocking chairs, thankful for the shade of the tin roof over the porch,
Barrentine leaned down to pet a stray cat drinking from a bucket.

My second question was more complicated, but it had been in my
mind since I interviewed Joe Gregory. Gregory told me about a strange
incident from the early 1980s. Kennedy didn't remember it now, but
Gregory insisted it happened. A few years before the Swain case, Kennedy and Gregory arrested two men they caught tending to an isolated
marijuana field. One of the men surprised the detectives by saying that
DA Glenn Thomas would have them out of jail within twenty-four
hours. A day later, the men were out of jail, the charges dropped. These
men were tied to the same band of drug traffickers as Barrentine. I'd
heard stories about his compatriots bribing officials to halt investiga-

tions, and I wondered whether Barrentine himself had gotten out of the Swain case with a bribe to an official.

I asked Barrentine. He said he knew of some officials who were corrupt in that era, but he didn't know much of anything about DA Thomas. He told me he was just a worker in the trafficking operation; he wasn't a boss. A bribe would have been above his pay grade.

But did someone try it in this case? I asked. Even if Barrentine didn't pay off the DA, someone else could've.

He thought for a moment, looking me in the eye off and on.

Possible, he said.

I asked him if he knew Erik Sparre. He said he didn't.

It was hard to know what to make of Donnie Barrentine. He seemed to love to tell stories, and he was good at it. He wasn't cagey—he revealed things. He told me that immediately after his arrest for possession of a machine gun in 1985, he scolded the Telfair County sheriff for taking part in the case because the sheriff was allegedly cozy with traffickers, saying, *You're in the same damn business as me.* Barrentine told me about the time his late cousin Greg Barrentine had buried tens of thousands of dollars on his property in Brantley County right before everyone in the crew got arrested. Donnie said no one ever got a chance to go back to claim the treasure. He told me about a homicide where he'd been suspected of killing a man—but this wasn't one of the cases where his suspect status was public knowledge. He said he was innocent, but still. Who offers something like that to a reporter?

Barrentine reminded me of muddy water. It was hard to know what was really under there, what was driving him. I wondered if he wanted to darken the water for just that reason. Did he want people to think he was full of it so they would disregard any incriminating information he let slip? Or did he, like so many charismatic people from the same part of the world as me, just love to hear himself talk so much that he couldn't help revealing things?

Before I drove away, Barrentine walked up to my car window. He said he hoped Dennis Perry could get some relief if he's innocent. But he cautioned me that after nearly thirty-five years, even if Perry wasn't the murderer, it was going to be tough to prove.

I COULDN'T SPEAK WITH SPARRE'S EX, EMILY HEAD. SHE'D BEEN murdered, shot in her rural Camden County home in 2013. The case, which Dale Bundy helped investigate, went cold. Investigators said the scene didn't look like a home invasion; it seemed like she'd let the killer inside. "It was spic and span," a sheriff's captain told *The Brunswick News*. "There was little evidence. There was a whole lot of nothing."

Sparre was questioned in the case but had an alibi and was cleared.

In 2018, another man, a state prisoner serving life for rapes in Savannah, was indicted for Emily Head's murder on charges including murder and burglary. He'd been connected to the crime by DNA, but it was unclear how or why he would've killed Head. There was no known connection between them, and Head lived in a neighborhood that you'd have to be lost to end up in.

Emily Head's family still wondered if Sparre was involved in her murder. I went to the Head family home and was greeted by Head's elderly mother. It was pouring rain, and we stood at the door under the overhang. When I mentioned the Swain murders and Sparre, she went quiet and did not invite me inside. Her soft smile turned into a blank expression. She said she didn't know anything and didn't want to be involved. Her daughter's murder case was complication enough for her life. Emily's twin brother Emmett came to the door and said he didn't want to be any part of the case either. He asked me to leave. From police documents, I knew that this family must've had many things to say about Sparre, a man who had allegedly harassed and menaced them and Emily for years. Walking back to the car, pelted by the rain, I felt for Head's mom and brother and wondered if they were still worried about Sparre.

I hoped for better luck with Sparre's second ex-wife, Rhonda.

When I knocked on her door several days later, Rhonda Tyson cracked the door and asked if she could help me. Her voice was wispy and high—imagine if a cat could speak and had grown up in Savannah. She was in her early fifties and seemed tired, like she'd had many strangers show up at her door about terrible things. Tyson had married Sparre in the months after Emily left him in 1985. As with Emily, Sparre had beaten Tyson, she told police. And Sparre had gotten away with it. In the early 1990s, she filed for divorce, and nowadays she tried to interact with him as little as possible, though it was difficult because they had two children together.

I told Tyson who I was, that I was reporting on something she might know about.

Is it about my son? she asked.

Rhonda and Erik's son, David Sparre, was the youngest person on death row in Florida. In 2010, the twenty-year-old went to Jacksonville for a week to take care of his grandma who was having surgery at a local hospital. During the trip, David met a twenty-one-year-old Black woman on Craigslist and met her for a date. Afterward, he went back to her apartment and pulled a knife on her. She tried to fight. He stabbed her eighty-nine times. Later in jail, he wrote a letter to his ex-girlfriend explaining that he'd previously killed someone else—he didn't say who—with a gun but murdered the woman in Jacksonville to see how it felt to kill with a knife. "I'm not even going to lie. I enjoyed it and I hope to do it again," David Sparre wrote. I'd read the letter before stopping by.

No, I told Tyson, *I want to talk about your son's dad.*

Her eyes grew wide, and she invited me in. We sat on an over-stuffed leather couch as Tyson's nine-year-old daughter played in the next room. We tried to keep our voices low.

Right away, Tyson started telling me about alleged abuse. She said that Erik Sparre cracked her cheekbone, caused more bruises and black eyes than she could count. Once, she said, he put a 9mm handgun in her mouth. She didn't know it wasn't loaded. He pulled the trigger, echoing an incident his first ex-wife accused him of. After leaving Sparre, Tyson slept with a knife under her pillow for nine years. She called herself a survivor, and after several decades of recovery, she no longer lived in fear.

When I asked what Erik Sparre had said about the church murders, she paused, gathering her thoughts for a long time, hands on a pillow on her lap. The silence almost hurt; I felt my anxiety rising.

"I wanna get it right. I don't want it to be misconstrued. I want to say what he said to me in the right way," she said. "I can remember him talking about it in pieces." She said she'd blocked out a lot of her memories of him.

I asked if Sparre was racist. Another long pause. "I believe in every cell of his body he is racist."

A few minutes later, Tyson spoke again. "I do remember him saying something about those—" she paused, debating how to phrase it, "N-words in the church and enjoying [killing them]." Tyson didn't remember Sparre saying why he did it, but she knew he was hateful, mean, and "had pure evil in his heart." Tyson said Sparre got those beliefs from his dad.

What about her son? She said that David had always been a normal enough kid until he spent a summer with his father. After that, he came back talking about Vikings and racial purity. After his arrest,

David told Tyson something else his dad had taught him. "My son told me Erik taught him to meet someone online, meet publicly with them, get comfortable with them, then go to their house, see what kind of valuables they have and rob them," Tyson said. After mutilating the young woman in Jacksonville, David Sparre stole a Sony PlayStation from her apartment and drove away in her car. In the jailhouse letter, he mentioned that before the murder, he'd taken some time to try to construct the "perfect alibi."

Thirty years before, Erik Sparre had a seemingly perfect alibi of his own. After the church murders, Joe Gregory checked out Sparre's alibi about working in the Brunswick Winn-Dixie. Sparre's boss confirmed that Sparre had been on the clock when the Swains died. But one part of the boss's statement, which Gregory detailed in his report, struck me as odd. "I have also talked with employees who are still working here who worked with Sparre that night," the man said. "They also confirmed that Sparre was in the store on that evening."

Gregory had called Sparre's manager in March 1986, a full year after the murders. I couldn't tell you where I was a year ago on a random night, let alone where a coworker was. My instinct told me there was something off here. I needed to talk to this boss, Donald A. Mobley.

At the newspaper, we used a program called LexisNexis to look up people through public records. We could find phone numbers, addresses, email addresses, employment, and so on. If your dad had a fishing license in 1992, LexisNexis probably knows. Yet I couldn't find anything to show that a Donald Mobley had ever lived anywhere near Brunswick.

I turned to archives of *The Brunswick News*, searching for stories or ads that mentioned the same Winn-Dixie in the mid-1980s. No results for Mobley, but I found the name of an employee who I hoped would've known Mobley. The employee was dead. With his obituary,

I found his widow, who said she couldn't help me but gave me a name. One person led to another. They seemed to think I was strange. Maybe they were right, but I kept calling, bothering so many widows. Finally, I had the name of a man who may have worked with Sparre and Mobley at Winn-Dixie in 1985.

He told me he'd never heard of Donald Mobley. His wife, who had also worked at the store, hadn't either. But they did know *David* Mobley. He managed the store back then, they said.

This made my heart pump faster and my skin get clammy. What if the GBI agent had just written down the wrong first name and Sparre really did have an alibi?

I asked the couple if they could help me find David Mobley. I said it was important. I was investigating the Rising Daughter Baptist Church murders, I told them, and the man serving life for the crime might be innocent. They gave me the phone number. In their driveway, I dialed.

David Mobley told me he managed the Winn-Dixie from 1981 to June 1986. He said the name Erik Sparre rang only the faintest bell. He remembered the church murders because the story was so shocking and terrible. But he had no memory of ever speaking to the police about an employee's whereabouts on the night of the murders. He would remember that, he insisted; the church murders were huge news. Did he have an employee named Donald Mobley? No, David said, he was the only Mobley who worked there. "I'm positive nobody in that store was named Donald Mobley."

But maybe David Mobley really *couldn't* remember a phone call that happened thirty-four years earlier. Later, I sat down in my hotel room with my laptop. On LexisNexis, I checked David Mobley's personal details against those listed for Donald Mobley on the GBI report.

If the agent had gotten Mobley's first name wrong, he also had his middle initial wrong.

And his home address.

And his birth date.

And his social security number.

And his home number.

And his work number.

None of them were even close.

Through old telephone directories at a local library, I found that the phone numbers listed for Mobley's work and home belonged to different people when Gregory wrote the report. Oddly, in 1986 the work number, which ought to have belonged to Winn-Dixie, belonged to a widow's home in Brunswick. Her daughter told me she had never heard of Donald Mobley or Erik Sparre. She said there was a phone in the back shed of the home, which people from a nearby halfway house had been caught using without permission.

Where did Gregory get the number to the Winn-Dixie? He said he didn't remember but said sometimes he would ask suspects for bosses' phone numbers back in the days before Google.

Then I told Gregory something I learned from Sparre's ex-wife Rhonda: Sparre used to change his voice and pretend to be other people on the phone. Gregory sounded crestfallen. Then I asked: Is it possible the person he spoke to all those years ago wasn't a Winn-Dixie manager at all?

"That's very possible," Gregory said

20

"I Need Your Help"

On a rainy October afternoon, Kennedy and I were back at the park on the Satilla River, under the pavilion roof. Kennedy studied Gregory's report about Sparre's alibi. He read to himself in a whisper. He finished, placed the paper on the picnic table, and set his blue eyes on my face as I went line by line, explaining how I'd learned that Sparre's alibi couldn't be verified.

Kennedy opened his mouth, but all that came out was a loud, sickened sound: "Oh, oh, oh, oh." The air from his lips caught the edge of the paper. The sheet lifted and danced across the table, back toward me. "God!" Kennedy said in anguish, slapping both knees with his palms, staring into the storm clouds over the river. "He's been in prison all this time. Oh, my God . . ."

Kennedy had stopped drinking four years ago, at age seventy. He started reading the Bible instead. He kept saying he wanted to live to see this case resolved. He thanked me for finding something he missed. "It may be something that takes this guy out of prison," he said. "*God almighty*. It just seems like it opens up a whole new door."

———

"HI MR. SPARRE," MY LETTER BEGAN. "I AM A REPORTER AT *THE Atlanta Journal-Constitution* newspaper and am working on a story that involves you."

I'd had trouble finding a phone number for Sparre and had been repeatedly admonished not to go to his home, which was allegedly full of guns, for my safety. I wanted to meet him in person, in a public place. I decided to start with a certified letter, which required a signature, to be sure he received it.

Within a few days Sparre opened my letter and began to read:

> The reason the story involves you is that your late ex-wife Emily came forward to police one year after the murders and let them hear a recording she said was you on the phone. The voice said: 'I'm the mother fucker that killed the two n———— in that church and I'm going to kill you and the whole damn family if I have to do it in church,' according to a police report. Emily also said you had lost your glasses around the time of the murders. A pair of glasses turned up at the murder scene. A police officer showed Emily three pairs of glasses and asked if any were the ones you lost. She picked the pair from the church.

I told him I was having trouble verifying his alibi.

"So I need your help," I wrote. "Could we set up a time to meet?"

Sparre called me. He sounded agitated over the phone. Best I could tell, no one had asked Sparre about the murders in thirty-three years—not until he opened my letter. He said he didn't kill the Swains, didn't even know them. He said he never told anyone he killed them. When I reminded him that he was caught on tape taking credit for the murder to his ex-wife's family, he denied it.

"What is the point of all this," he asked, exacerbated. "The police investigated. They searched my house. When they realized my ex-wife said that because she was mad, they charged me with terroristic threats." He sped through excuses. "I don't even know where the church is, even though I'm from over there," he said, referring to Rising Daughter Baptist Church—one of the only structures that isn't a home or barn in Spring Bluff. "Like I said, I do not know the Swains. Never met them. The rumors I heard at the time that went on is that that guy was involved in some kind of dope trade and basically wasn't going to pay them for it. That was the rumor going around at the time. I don't even remember who told me that."

He was breathing heavier.

"Do you know," I asked, "why they didn't charge you?"

"Because I *didn't do it.*"

Sparre remembered being interrogated by Joe Gregory and Sheriff Smith. He remembered hearing that Dennis Perry was charged and said he hoped he was guilty. I heard him light a cigarette. He brought up his son on death row and suggested that his son's case had changed the father. He told me about his garden, how he liked to watch life grow, not tear it down. He said what his son did had nothing to do with him, and that if I thought this was a "like father, like son" situation, I was wrong. David Sparre killed—*not* Erik Sparre. Erik said he used to have Black friends in Spring Bluff.

"Look, dude, I really don't want any part of this," he said.

I said that was OK, but could we just meet so I could tell him what I learned? I suggested a restaurant down the highway from his house. He said he'd prefer to meet at his home, way out in Brantley County. I told him the restaurant was better for me, and he said he'd consider it.

IN THE MEANTIME, PERRY'S ATTORNEYS WERE SEARCHING FOR new evidence to shake things loose. After learning about Sparre's faulty

alibi, the attorneys had an investigator follow Sparre in hopes of finding a discarded DNA sample, such as from a cigarette butt. They'd
tried this before without luck, but they had to try again. A DNA
match was still possible, even though the evidence from the crime
scene was over thirty years old. The glasses found at the crime scene,
which were pieced together from multiple pairs and bore marks that
appeared from welding or working on cars, were gone, and so were the
two hairs stuck in the hinge. Luckily, the hair had been tested ahead
of Perry's trial, and the genetic code was written out in the case file.
Because of the limitations on DNA tests at the time, only mitochondrial DNA could be extracted from the sample. This meant that the
DNA profile couldn't be used to pinpoint just one donor. Instead,
it could be used to match anyone in the same maternal line. Dennis
Perry, Donnie Barrentine, and several men tied to Barrentine's gang
weren't a match with the hair sample. But Sparre hadn't been tested.

The investigator followed Sparre around for days without noticing
him leaving behind anything that could be tested for DNA. Finally,
he threw a Hail Mary. He stopped by Sparre's home while Sparre was
at work. Sparre lived with his elderly mother. The investigator arrived
with a brand-new pair of scissors and told Sparre's mother who he
was, that he was investigating the church murders and wanted to
make sure her son hadn't done it. The investigator said that all they
needed to do was test the hair of anyone in Sparre's maternal line.

I know my son didn't do this, Gladys Sparre said.

She let the investigator snip a lock of her hair. Before long, it was
on its way to a lab. Perry's attorneys told no one—including me—that
they were doing a DNA test.

AT THE TIME, MY FOCUS WAS STILL ON MEETING SPARRE TO
discuss his alibi. To my surprise, he agreed to meet at the restau-

rant. Hoping to quell my sources' and editors' concerns of a confrontation, I decided to bring along a photographer from the paper who'd worked in war zones. As I tried to align our schedules, my phone rang.

Sparre, sounding panicked again and angry, accused me of coming to his house and taking a clipping of his mother's hair for a DNA test. He said I pretended to be a GBI agent. He said he knew it was me because the GBI would leave a card, and this man hadn't left a card. My jaw fell open as I realized, but kept to myself, that Perry's attorneys must have arranged this.

"It damn sure wasn't me," I said.

Sparre said he was done talking with me. I heard him spit in the dirt.

"This DNA will prove that I didn't do it."

THE DNA DID NOT PROVE THAT.

The test showed that the hairs from the crime scene belonged to someone in Sparre's maternal line: 99.6 percent of the North American population would not be a match; Sparre was.

For Dennis and Brenda Perry, the news brought tears of joy. Dennis called it an answered prayer and told his attorneys he felt like a free man already—he just needed the system, the broken, lumbering system, to catch up.

The news thrilled Kennedy. "Prayer does work," he said when one of Perry's lawyers called to tell him. Kennedy knew people would ask why he and Gregory didn't test Sparre when they investigated him in 1986. The reason was simple: it wasn't done back then. He and Gregory had probably never even heard of DNA testing, pioneered the same year as the murders.

That didn't stop Kennedy from blaming himself. He recognized that the DNA could be the best evidence yet that he and Gregory failed in the investigation. They'd had Sparre. They had let him go. That realization was crushing.

IN LATE MARCH, THE GEORGIA INNOCENCE PROJECT TOOK THE DNA results to Brunswick Judicial Circuit district attorney Jackie Johnson. Jackie Johnson could've considered the evidence and asked a judge to free Perry, as other prosecutors had done when new testing brought convictions into question. But she declined to do so and chose not to start an investigation into the new evidence. Four legal experts—a former prosecutor, a defense attorney, a criminal justice professor, and a former Georgia Supreme Court justice—told me that unless the DA had bombshell evidence to refute the DNA, she should move to free Perry. These sources were surprised by the DA's decision, but after they considered her reputation, it made more sense.

On April 27, 2020, the Georgia Innocence Project filed an extraordinary motion for a new trial. "The new DNA evidence is critically significant because it for the first time provides reliable forensic physical evidence linking a known suspect, Erik Sparre, to physical evidence at the crime scene," the lawyers wrote. They argued that Perry never would have been prosecuted had Sparre's DNA been tested in 2001 along with other suspects in the run-up to the trial. If the DNA match had come to light before the trial, the petition said, the state "almost certainly" would've built a case against Sparre.

On the day of the filing, my first story on the case ran in *The Atlanta Journal-Constitution*. Before publishing, I called Sparre, but he told me he didn't want to talk. "I'm not going to sit here and go into all this. You got your DNA thing. That was you that came by and got that," Sparre told me. I said that his mother's hair had been taken by the Georgia Innocence Project. I told him the DNA was a match to hairs in the glasses found next to the bodies. "I want to see how you can explain that," I said.

"Look, I have no idea," he said. "I don't have any glasses missing."

I told him that in 1986 his ex-wife told police that he had a pair like the ones found at the church.

"I don't know what she told them—and I don't care," he said, raising his voice. "I want to be left alone. Leave me alone. Do not call me anymore." He hung up.

AFTER MY FIRST STORY WAS PUBLISHED, I ALSO CALLED CYNTHIA Clayton to check in. She was shocked and deeply confused. "I'm not sure what's what," she said. "I don't understand the situation with the hair samples and all that."

It had been thirty-five years since her aunt and uncle were murdered. Yet somehow there was still so much uncertainty, still reporters calling her with new information. The man in prison for the murders might be innocent? And the real killer might be a white supremacist who lived nearby? It was too much to process. Clayton decided to wait and see what the DA's office would tell her before she formed her opinion.

Meanwhile, the DA was busy with mounting outrage over another homicide case that would soon become international news.

21

More Blood, More Reckoning

In February 2020, Ahmaud Arbery, a twenty-five-year-old Black man, went jogging outside Brunswick. He had struck out on an afternoon run in a neighborhood called Satilla Shores, near the Sidney Lanier Bridge—which, as it happened, Erik Sparre had helped build. Within moments, a white resident called 911. He suspected, without evidence, that Arbery was behind the recent burglaries in his neighborhood. Impatient and emboldened by his deep connections in local law enforcement, the man and his adult son drove after Arbery in their truck, planning to make a citizen's arrest. Arbery didn't see them at first. Then another white neighbor joined the pursuit. The leader, a recently retired investigator with the Brunswick DA's office, stood in the back of his pickup with a handgun trained on Arbery's back. The man's stance looked like he was chasing down an enemy in a war or hunting. His son, armed with a shotgun, was driving. The neighbor following them started recording with his cell phone.

Within two minutes of Arbery stepping out of his home, he heard the men screaming for him to stop. Arbery turned around to find three random white men in trucks following him with guns—he wasn't stopping.

He tried to duck them, sprinting down different streets as they hollered. He ran for ten more minutes until the leading truck cut him off in the middle of the road. The investigator's son climbed out with his shotgun. Arbery, surely fearing he'd be shot, went for the gun, and the man squeezed the trigger. The twenty-five-year-old hit the ground, bleeding.

As he lay dying, the shooter said: "Fucking n———."

The murder made the local paper—as a death with no charges filed—in a short article with few details. The case only gained more attention when calls from Arbery's family and area residents forced further investigation. In the weeks after the shooting, officials released next to no information, angering locals who started to put pressure on DA Jackie Johnson. Johnson recused herself from the investigation because one of the suspects had worked for her. But she was facing growing criticism for allegedly telling police not to arrest anyone before she punted the case to the DA in Waycross, George Barnhill.

Barnhill watched Arbery's horrifying last moments on the cell phone video and concluded that the white men had done nothing wrong. Arbery's killers, Barnhill said, were protected by Georgia's Civil War–era citizen's arrest law, the same law that had been used against Black people fleeing bondage. Some two hundred years after Arbery's Gullah Geechee ancestors remade their lives on Cumberland Island and forged the first community owned by freed people in the United States, the laws of the slave era were still being weaponized. The tide was always coming back here.

Brunswick activists banded together in mourning and fury, organizing protests and community meetings.

Then on May 5, 2020, the cell phone video leaked, sparking outrage across the country and the world. Presidential candidate Joe Biden—and countless others—called it a lynching. Georgia's Republican governor and attorney general denounced the murder and vowed a state investigation of prosecutors' handling of the case. Arbery's face, painted on murals and printed on shirts, became another symbol of the Black Lives Matter movement. Days after the video emerged, the GBI created a task force to investigate the case—and filed murder charges within hours.

Although DA Johnson escaped the worst of the fallout from Arbery's murder, she continued to face scorn over the Perry case. Weeks after Arbery's video went public, I followed up my initial piece with an eleven-thousand-word story, printed in a special section in the newspaper, accompanied by a documentary made by my filmmaker colleagues, brothers Ryon and Tyson Horne, and others at the *AJC*. Days later, in early June, Johnson finally asked the GBI to investigate the Swain case. This was extraordinary: the reopening of a thirty-five-year-old double murder case while a man the GBI had helped convict sat in prison for the crime. It was unheard of in modern Georgia history. The GBI assembled a task force of nearly a dozen agents from around the state, including many of the same agents on the Arbery task force.

MEANWHILE, I WAS STILL REPORTING AND TALKING WITH ANYone I could who knew Erik Sparre. Driving up and down I-95 through multiple states, I visited women he'd been in relationships with and found that many remained afraid of Sparre's wrath. One would only barely crack the door, spooked by the mere mention of his name. She said he'd bragged about belonging to the Ku Klux Klan. Another woman was terrified that I'd been able to find her. She paced her yard as a relative explained that she was afraid of Sparre finding her. If I found her, why couldn't he? I tried to reassure her, explaining that I had resources and experience as a journalist that he didn't, but a car came and took the woman away.

I spoke with his former coworkers, neighbors, and friends and noticed a striking pattern. Typically, when I'd brought up racism to white people in South Georgia, I got rolled eyes and ribbing—*Quit playing the race card*. But when I asked about Sparre, these people didn't hesitate: *Yes, very racist*. One person recalled how he screamed the N-word in an argument with a small group of Black folks at the Satilla River, waving a Confederate flag that Sparre, like more people than you'd think around here, had on him. I remembered how his ex-wife Rhonda Tyson had told me how their son, David, returned from a summer with his father transformed, obsessed with his Viking heritage. What else had the father and son talked about? I decided to try to reach David Sparre and sent a letter to his far-flung Florida prison.

I received this letter in return, handwritten in blue pen:

I start off by saying good day sir. What on God's green earth inspired you to write to me must have been awe-inspiring. The date of my birth is on the 7th day of the 7th month upon the 91st year of the 20th century. Therefore the vessel that contains my soul had not yet been created. My loyalty to my family knows no bounds. I would burn in hell for all eternity before I betray my family. I am the oldest son [he's not the oldest] of the oldest son, the only Sparre son to still carry the Sparre name. The blood of my ancestors who were Viking warriors flow [*sic*] through my veins. Whatever makes you think I would betray my father in such a way as you suggested? I do not fear death nor God nor Lucifer.

Respectfully, David Sparre —X.

In the postscript, he reiterated: "I love my father. I will not turn on him. Find another who will."

IT HAD BEEN SIX MONTHS SINCE I WATCHED DALE BUNDY STOMP away, refusing to speak with me at the sheriff's office. I assumed he'd read my stories with the revelations about DNA evidence and Sparre's alibi. He must have thoughts about the case. I called him, asking if he wanted to talk.

"Absolutely—," he said, coughing. "Absolutely not."

He said that Joe Gregory had lied to me. Bundy didn't say about what. He said if I needed any information about the case, I should contact prosecutor John Johnson. (Johnson wasn't related to DA Johnson.) I mentioned that Johnson hadn't been responding to my messages other than to say he had a personal policy about speaking on old cases—a stunning policy for a man who dealt with matters of life and death, one I'd never heard of another prosecutor having.

"What do you think of the DNA evidence?"

"Well," Bundy said, "I think it's mitochondrial DNA. . . . It doesn't identify a person. It just identifies a family line it can go all the way back to Eve in the Garden of Eden. I congratulate you on your efforts, but it is what it is."

He told me, as he'd told *Undisclosed*, that he dropped Sparre as a suspect because Sparre had told his wife that he'd killed the Swains with a shotgun, "which absolutely is not what happened in church." I asked where he got that information, because it wasn't mentioned in any police report, or even in the stories told by his ex-wives and others who knew Erik Sparre. Bundy insisted that the shotgun detail should be in a report somewhere. "But anyway, I've been told not to speak to you about this. And if you would kindly refer any more contact over to John Johnson and don't call me again at home, I would appreciate it. I'm retired now, put all this back behind me."

He didn't mention that he'd retired immediately after I left his office. In this call, Bundy was much calmer than he had been when I first met him.

"I'm sorry I was so rude that day," said Bundy, who had also apologized to Susan Simpson for their last conversation. I thanked Bundy and accepted his apology.

LATE ONE NIGHT, AFTER WEEKS OF CHASING AFTER ANYONE who knew Erik Sparre, an email arrived in my inbox from a man named Kalem Head. "This article is pretty spot on as to what I've always been told," he wrote. "Erik [Sparre] is a horrible person and he has done some horrible things in his life. I am one of his many kids. Please keep looking into this guy and keep the pressure on him."

I knew who Kalem was from my reporting—a son Sparre had with his late ex-wife Emily Head—but I hadn't yet reached out. He was in his early thirties with a young family. He was, I would learn, one of about ten children Sparre had fathered by various women. When Kalem and I spoke over Zoom, he told me his father—he preferred to call him a sperm donor—hadn't been in his life at all. Sparre didn't so much as call him until he was eighteen years old. After that, Kalem changed his number. He wanted nothing to do with him.

Kalem hadn't always felt that way. When he was a kid, he used to pester his mother, Emily Head, by asking again and again, *Why don't I know my dad?* She found the softest way she could to tell the little boy that his father didn't want to be a father. She left out everything else. She kept dodging Kalem's questions until one day around the time of Perry's arrest, Emily finally told her son: Your father is a racist who beat women and, once, murdered two Black people in a church and got away with it. She said she had no idea why police had charged another man for the crime—Sparre had confessed on tape to the murders. If Emily Head ever told the police this next part, it was lost somehow; there is no known transcript of her interview. Kalem Head remembers his mother telling him about a night when Sparre came home with blood splashed on his clothes.

"He had blood all over his face," Kalem told me. "And she asked him what happened. He said, 'Don't worry about it. It's not your fucking business.'" The next day, she heard about the murders at Rising Daughter Baptist Church.

IN THE GATHERING STORM, SPARRE MOVED OUT OF THE HOME he shared with his elderly mother in Brantley County. He didn't want her to have to watch him go through the investigation. Sparre's brother and sister-in-law took him in. He receded into their Brunswick home, playing video games and watching TV while they were away at work. He stopped driving because his license had been revoked over unpaid child support; he'd allegedly driven without a license for years but now didn't want to give the GBI any extra opportunity to arrest him. He rarely spoke on the phone, worried that agents were listening in.

Agents were closing in on Sparre, interviewing people who knew him. They found that many had stories to tell. Sparre allegedly told one person, in addition to his first two wives, that he had killed the Swains. He allegedly told two people variations of the same statement, that he "killed some n——s back in my day." And Sparre had been heard taunting a Black man and suggesting he would kill him. *Are you ready to go meet your ancestors? I already sent two over there.* After agents learned this, they told the DA's office, which still didn't move to release Perry. Instead, prosecutors were preparing to argue that he should stay in prison. In an email to Perry's attorneys, Jackie Johnson revealed the position the state would take: Perry's conviction can't be overturned because twenty years earlier, to spare himself the death penalty, he'd waived his right to appeal.

ON THE MORNING OF JULY 13, DENNIS PERRY WAS LED INTO THE same dull, brightly lit prison office where he'd listened to each episode of *Undisclosed*. He looked gaunt and old in his baggy white jumpsuit as he blinked into a webcam. Due to COVID restrictions, he had to watch his hearing from prison. Only Perry's attorneys, the prosecutors, the head of the GBI task force, myself, and a few other reporters were in the courtroom, while Perry's loved ones watched in an overflow room. Phil Holladay, a veteran lawyer at the King & Spalding corporate law firm helping represent Perry pro bono, opened the hearing by describing the state's position. Prosecutors were about to argue to keep Perry locked in prison despite mounting evidence of his innocence. "Your Honor, the truth and Mr. Perry's twenty-plus-year quest for justice and his [motion for a new trial] deserve more than technical defenses, procedural roadblocks, and further delay." He said the evidence presented would show Perry's innocence resoundingly.

"These new DNA test results cannot be overlooked or downplayed," said Holladay. "They are a game changer in every sense of the word—not only as it relates to Mr. Perry's innocence in the slaying, but also . . . providing justice for the Swain family and to the perpetrator who did commit these horrific murders."

Andrew Ekonomou, a prosecutor who had recently represented President Donald Trump regarding Russian interference in the US election, said the hearing had nothing to do with anyone's guilt or innocence.

"It's [about] one simple thing: Should this court—can this court—

grant Mr. Perry's extraordinary motion for new trial? That's it," he said, indignant, looking up from his notes at a dark wood lectern. "This motion for new trial is barred by the doctrine of appeal waiver, your honor," Ekonomou went on. "Mr. Perry was convicted and stands convicted and is guilty today of the murder of Pastor [Harold was a deacon] and Mrs. Swain in their church in Camden County. He was found guilty by a jury in 2003." After the conviction, the state agreed to give up its "valuable right" to seek the death penalty, Ekonomou argued, in exchange for "any post-conviction rights to appeal or to challenge that conviction that he had."

At the prosecution table, John Johnson, who'd sent Perry away to prison, looked on approvingly. Ekonomou read from the trial transcript from 2003, noting where the judge had asked if Perry understood the deal and he said, "Yes, ma'am." With disdain in his voice, Ekonomou described how Perry had broken the agreement by filing a motion for a new trial and a habeas corpus. Ekonomou sought to bar the defense from calling witnesses, to shut the hearing down. His point boiled down to this: Whoever the killer really was, a deal is a deal.

The judge turned to Perry's lawyers and told them to start calling witnesses. Sparre's second ex-wife, Rhonda Tyson, took the stand, testifying that Sparre had told her in the late 1980s that he'd killed the Swains.

"I was laying on the floor, he was straddling me on my chest with his hands on my throat," Tyson said. Sparre allegedly said: "I will kill you like I killed those N-words in the church in Camden County."

Ekonomou asked Tyson why she hadn't mentioned in an affidavit that Sparre said the murders he committed were in a church. In the affidavit, she said Sparre said he killed two Black people in Camden County, but not specifically where the killings took place.

"Did you give that affidavit," said Ekonomou, handing Tyson a copy, and walking away from her. She said she did.

"Now you're saying today that he said it was in church," Ekonomou said, turning around to look right at her. "When you gave the affidavit, you just said Camden County."

"Yes."

"Which is it?"

"In the church in Camden County," said Tyson, who had told me that Sparre said the murders were in the church. That the words "in the church" were missing from an affidavit typed up by Perry's legal team amounted to a clerical error.

"Why didn't you say that?" the prosecutor said.

"There's a lot been going through my mind," said Tyson.

Reading pointedly from his copy of her affidavit, Ekonomou said, "You said he beat you up, stabbed you, cracked your cheekbone, broke your nose and all that. Why didn't you go to the police and explain that he had assaulted you and beat you up?"

"Because they did nothing the last time and the time before that," Tyson said.

Next, Chad Head, a brother of Sparre's late ex-wife Emily, was called to testify. He appeared virtually, calling in from his pickup truck. He said Sparre "stayed on drugs" in the mid-1980s and liked to beat on his sister. He said that Sparre's family owned some property behind the Head family home, and Sparre would shoot a gun from his side toward the Head home. "He would go down and he would shoot all day long," Head said.

"He always wanted to call us and threatened to shoot the place up or to kill somebody or something like that. It was pretty toxic." The family started recording the calls. Head recalled a time when Sparre called and said: "I'm the mother fucker who killed them n——s down there in the church, and I'm the mother fucker who's gonna come and kill y'all." After that, they contacted the sheriff's office. Butch Kennedy and Sheriff Smith came over to hear the tape. The police brought evidence with them, including glasses, Chad Head remembered, and his sister recognized a pair as belonging to Sparre.

What happened to the tape? Head said they gave it to the police. The prosecutors were grimacing.

The next witness, Jennifer Tyre, was more bad news for them. Tyre said she used to know Sparre through her ex-husband, who'd worked with him on the Sidney Lanier Bridge. Tyre had declined to speak with me and she was terribly nervous to testify after being subpoenaed.

Perry's attorney, Jennifer Whitfield, asked about Tyre's husband's birthday party in October 2000. Tyre said: "It's been so long ago that I don't even remember what conversation we were having or how it came up. Erik said to me that he had killed some Black persons, some N-words, in the past, and he would not be afraid to do it again."

The hearing—a stunning display that made the DA's office look incompetent or worse—ended with a sigh when the judge said he'd release his ruling later. He said it would be as early as that Friday—it was Monday—and that he would weigh the state's argument that Perry couldn't seek a new trial because of his appeal waiver. At Coffee Correctional Facility, Perry, mind reeling and outraged to hear the state fight the evidence against Sparre, was led away from the webcam, back to his cell.

AMID THE WAITING. BRENDA PERRY'S HOUSE NEAR WAVERLY, GEORGIA.
An unexpected visitor arrived at the rural home where Brenda lived with multiple generations of her family and, she hoped eventually, her husband, Dennis. It's a white ranch-style house with a chain-link fence to

keep the dogs—and grandkids—from running off down the dirt road or into the thick woods. The man who walked up the cement driveway had something awful on his heart.

Phillip Head, thirty-six, was burly with dark brown hair like the father he'd sworn off long ago. Head was friends with Brenda's son, Jabo, who lived next door. Head had read my stories about the church murders and the evidence tying his father to the crime. He told Brenda that he was there to apologize. Like his younger brother Kalem, Phillip didn't have a good relationship with Sparre, and he was devastated to learn what my stories had revealed about their father.

Phillip wanted to apologize for his blood—for what the man who happened to be his biological father allegedly did, and what it meant for Brenda and Dennis.

Brenda hugged him and thanked him.

22

A Decision and a Death

Shortly before the judge revealed his decision, I finally got John Johnson on the phone and asked a question I'd been wanting to ask him for months.

"Do you think Dennis Perry killed Harold and Thelma Swain?"

"Yes. Based on the evidence at trial, I do," said Johnson.

He said an innocent person could match the DNA from the crime scene, which meant Sparre could be innocent. Johnson evidently didn't know that because his office forgot to seal them, I had the same evidence from the GBI's investigation into Sparre that he did. In total, those recordings revealed that Sparre had made statements about killing two Black people to eleven people—nearly all of them separately, years apart. I didn't tell the prosecutor what I knew.

"Mr. Johnson," I said, losing my patience after almost a year of learning about the problems with Johnson's case against Perry, "are you a betting man? What are the odds? What are the odds?"

He didn't answer.

THE JUDGE DIDN'T BET ON JOHN JOHNSON. ON FRIDAY, JUDGE
Stephen Scarlett overturned Dennis Perry's convictions. In the ruling,
delivered to all parties in an email, he said that the record showed that
Perry had waived his rights to an appeal—not all post-conviction filings. The DA's office had presented a document that said Perry waived
all post-conviction rights, but Perry never even signed the form. It
would be a "miscarriage of justice," Scarlett wrote, to prevent the new
evidence from being heard. The case against Perry was "weak," the
judge said, compared to the new physical evidence on Sparre.

But the judge's order did not grant Perry's release. With his conviction gone, Perry still faced the original murder charges while the DA's
office decided whether to retry him. A retrial was all but impossible
because of the evidence against Sparre.

Perry felt unbelievable relief and joy when he heard of the ruling. But Brenda Perry struggled to balance the good news with the
disappointment that she didn't yet know when her husband could
come home.

"I don't know how to be excited," she said, starting to cry. "We
can't even share it."

She was also worried about the ongoing COVID outbreak in
the prison. There were more cases at Perry's facility than at any other
prison in Georgia. Perry's attorneys filed a motion for his immediate
release that day, Friday. The judge set a hearing on the issue for the
following Thursday.

BEFORE HEADING BACK TO ATLANTA, I CALLED CYNTHIA CLAY-
ton to check in. I hated how complex this whole process was for those
who knew and loved the Swains. They had generally thought, because
he'd been tried and convicted, that Perry was guilty. Clayton sounded
disheartened. She told me nicely but clearly that she didn't want to

comment or speak with reporters about the case anymore. It was all hard enough without having to field questions about what she was going through. I told her I understood. But the shock and pain wasn't over.

ON SUNDAY MY PHONE RANG. IT WAS A KEY SOURCE.

Josh, she said, *you need to get out of your house.*

What?

You need to go somewhere. Can you go somewhere?

I asked her to explain why. She said she couldn't. She implored me to hang up and go to a hotel. I asked if it had something to do with Sparre. She said she couldn't say, but the way she hesitated made me think it did. I called one of my editors who told me to pack a bag and leave. I climbed in my car and drove to a CVS parking lot when my phone rang. It was Sparre's son Kalem Head.

Erik's mother was found murdered, he said.

I yelled in shock and anger. I pounded the steering wheel. Across Georgia and Florida, witnesses were having similar reactions.

Gladys Sparre had last been seen three days earlier—on the day Perry's conviction was overturned based largely on a DNA sample she'd provided. Typically, on Sunday mornings, a friend from church would come pick her up to attend the service. That day, the friend found Gladys Sparre, seventy-nine, dead on the bathroom floor.

Still stunned, I checked into a hotel near Atlanta and wondered how long I'd be there. My bosses—and *AJC* security—told me I had to stay at least until they felt it was safe to return home. I started making calls to sources, and my phone was ringing nonstop as word spread through social media. The rumor was that Gladys Sparre had been found with a bag over her head.

Erik Sparre was being questioned by the GBI. He said he hadn't seen his mother and hadn't been to the house. His brother, Peter Sparre, vouched for him—as did video from a security system on Peter's house. Erik hadn't left the house in days. In a televised interview, Peter said his brother hadn't done anything to their mother. The brothers had been together since she had last been seen alive, he said. He defended Erik in the Swain investigation, as well, saying there was no evidence Erik had faked his alibi.

That night, I called Eve Rogers, the high-ranking GBI analyst heading the task force investigating the church murders. She suggested that the bag—wrapping from hygiene products—wasn't over the woman's head as much as touching it. It could've been there before she fell. Rogers said that nothing at the scene appeared amiss, and there were no signs of trauma.

"My gut right now is that we're not going to know much until we hear back from the autopsy," she said, sounding exhausted. "And truly it could be natural, it could be a suicide, it could be a murder. There's obviously some strange circumstances that make you scratch your head. But nothing definitive either one way or the other."

The GBI was keeping eyes on Sparre. Meanwhile, witnesses who'd spoken with me, the Georgia Innocence Project, and the GBI task force were worried. They had left their homes or contacted their local police or sheriff's office and asked to have a security check on their homes. When they explained the circumstances, agencies quickly obliged.

The autopsy was inconclusive. The GBI decided to run toxicology and other tests. But with the agency's notoriously backed-up crime lab, those tests would take weeks if not months. In the meantime, the agency had no reason to hold or charge Erik Sparre. Over the next few days, witnesses started going back to their homes. I went home, too. Then I headed south from Atlanta again for Perry's bond hearing.

ON THURSDAY, JULY 23, BRENDA PERRY FELT HER MIND TUMBLING in worry. It was the morning of the hearing, and Brenda had to watch from outside due to COVID restrictions, so she assembled with a couple dozen friends and relatives outside the Brunswick courthouse. It felt like a family reunion or a cookout—or if you looked into Brenda's eyes, maybe a funeral.

Prosecutors had said they wouldn't oppose Perry's release on bond, but Brenda had no reason to trust them. Brenda worried that prosecutors might ask for the judge to banish Dennis from Camden County, which Brenda and her family had always called home. Perry's cousin, Suzanne, cued up the video feed on her cell phone.

"He's on," she said.

Brenda waved, singing, "Heeeeey, baby." Dennis, heavily pixelated, waved back.

A bewildered-looking young man appeared on their screens—a prosecutor who'd been sent to surrender. The prosecutors who'd fought to send Perry to prison, and keep him there, were not at this man's side. "First and foremost, your honor," said the prosecutor, "we understand the situation and . . ."—he glanced down at his paper-strewn desk, evidently searching for the least embarrassing way to phrase it for his bosses—"agree that Mr. Perry is in need of a bond at this point."

The DA's office requested a $10,000 bond, which would require Brenda to put up the house. She was prepared to do it.

"Banish . . . ," Brenda heard the prosecutor say, and her body grew tense. A friend held onto her in one long hug. The prosecutor said that the DA's office wanted Perry banished from Camden County.

Perry's attorney Jennifer Whitfield appeared on-screen, looking like she was trying not to scowl, smile, and cry at the same time: "Mr. Dennis Perry is a fifty-eight-year-old man. He's a loving husband. He's known as Papa Sunshine to his grandchildren. He has no history of violence in his fifty-eight years," she said. "Mr. Perry has been wrongfully imprisoned"—and she pounded each of these next words to drive the point—"*For. Over. Twenty. Years.* The concept of banishment in this case—," she said, stopping when she heard the judge interrupt.

"He's not gonna be banished," he said.

The judge said he'd let Perry go without bond. He would be released as soon as staff at the prison could finish all the paperwork, which Whitfield had pressed them to start early. Perry would be free in a few hours.

When the judge finished, Perry spoke up: "Thank you, your honor," he said, barely stopping his tears.

Brenda was sobbing and sniffling while others stifled cheers, trying not to interrupt the hearing. Brenda turned to her great-grandson, Bubba, the eight-year-old who'd been trailing her all morning. "We can go get Papa Sunshine today," Brenda said.

"There's only one thing I have to say," Bubba said. "Hallelujah."

"God is good," said the grandmother who had struggled so often to fully believe that.

SEVERAL HOURS LATER, A LOUD CLANK RANG OVER THE PRISON parking lot: the sound of something coming loose. The gate crept open, and Dennis Perry stepped out. He raised a hand in triumph, laughing, glowing. His attorneys and family cheered.

Dennis and Brenda went for each other in one fast move. They kissed through face masks. Before now, the guards had never let the husband and wife touch for more than four or five seconds. Dennis took Brenda into his arms, and she took him into hers, for five seconds, ten. They didn't speak. For fifteen seconds, twenty. They listened to each other breathe. They cried. People hollered and clapped, smiling with tears in their eyes. When the couple let go, it had been thirty-five seconds.

The Perrys posed in front of the Coffee Correctional Facility sign, surrounded by pink rosebushes. They didn't want a picture to remember the place—they were posing to prove that Perry and his family had made it out of its grip.

Perry didn't mind answering a few questions from the scrum of reporters crowded around him.

"Dennis, did you ever think this day would come?"

"Yeah," he said almost immediately, and then his voice was swamped with emotion. "I told my wife I was gonna pray myself out of here. And that's what I've done." He looked up. "Because I asked God for some help." He squinted away tears, stared down at the grass. "It's OK," Brenda whispered in his ear.

"I just wanna go home now," Perry said.

Headed to the car, he saw that his wife had followed through with her promise to bring him sweet tea and boiled peanuts. He cackled in excitement. A few hours later, he arrived to the home he'd only seen in pictures. Perry stood in the driveway, smiling like somebody who knew they'd earned some happiness. He leaned on the side of the SUV, catching up with his dear friend and former prison bunk-mate, John. They'd feared the system would keep them from seeing each other again after John's parole, and now they grinned together. In the house, dinner was cooking: tomatoes and rice with sausage, like Dennis hoped.

Perry had asked me to stop by. He wanted to thank me. So did Brenda, her daughter-in-law, and all of their numerous relatives, blood and otherwise, who were passing through. I thanked them for thanking me. But I had trouble focusing on anything but this: Dennis looked *at home*. Not just like he belonged here—but like he'd always been here. He had in some ways. He was thought of more often here, his name more often invoked here, than some people who'd actually lived here. Dennis had just caught up physically. I kept wondering what he would feel when the buzz wore off and he reckoned with twenty years of captivity.

For now, every time I looked over at him, he was smiling, surrounded by people who loved him and had waited to see him delivered home.

PERRY'S FIRST DAYS WERE FILLED WITH A MIX OF WONDER AND grief—wonder for how the world and his life had changed, grief for all the people who didn't live to see his freedom. Sometimes his emotions felt out of control. Therapy would help with that. But there were moments when he felt utterly alive. His first time back to the Satilla River, he cried in joy. He jumped in. He jumped back into the life he should have been enjoying for decades. He and Brenda took road trips, went to church and met people. They were always together, except for when Brenda was at work running the high school cafeteria, but Dennis would call her on her way there and back home. It felt more natural to talk on the phone than in person, because of their experience. Time would work on that. At night, when Dennis would grill their dinner, they'd turn up old country love songs and slow dance.

A COUPLE OF MONTHS AFTER PERRY'S RELEASE, A CONVOY OF GBI vehicles drove through the backwoods of Brantley County toward Waynesville. Nearly twenty agents drove onto Erik Sparre's property. They entered the home, a green barn-looking structure that he built himself, and began looking through drawers, closets, and the loft. They pulled boxes out of a large storage shed and sifted through, pulling out postcards, pictures, documents, writings—and photographed them on folding tables under tents.

In the storage building, they found two cannons—icons for Civil War buffs—about two feet high and seemingly functional. A member of the task force picked up a long-sleeved dress shirt that was on a hanger in the shed. The shirt was one big Confederate flag. Agents searched the ground with metal detectors. After the search concluded, an agent placed a copy of the search warrant on the front door. They'd found a lot on Erik Sparre's property, but nothing that definitively linked him to the Swains' murders or to his mother's death.

The GBI's blood tests couldn't determine what killed Gladys Sparre. Some people who knew her thought she might've accidentally poisoned herself. She'd been diagnosed with dementia recently, and after a period without serious issues, she started having more trouble with her mind. At the same time, she ran out of one of her medications and noticed that an over-the-counter insect killer contained an ingredient with a similar name. She supposedly rubbed the poison on her skin, causing rashes, and had to seek medical help. Just a few weeks later, she was found dead.

THE GBI TASK FORCE WAS WORN OUT AND FRUSTRATED. SURE, many people had heard Sparre brag about carrying out the Swain murders. But after nearly four decades, a trial against him could be difficult. They wanted more evidence. Agents found Sparre arrogant and flippant about the allegations. But he must have felt the pressure, the sheer isolation and terror of being a suspect in a double murder. He'd abandoned his life and retreated into his brother and sister-in-law's house. Sparre had no idea how much evidence the task force had amassed. Sparre's brother and sister-in-law took him to Florida for a trip. They must've feared this could be their last outing together. Soon, Erik could be charged. At nearly sixty, a murder conviction almost certainly meant that he would die in prison.

AFTER DARK ONE NIGHT, GBI AGENTS DESCENDED UPON THE house and took Sparre away for an interrogation. Was this the moment he never came home again? The agents questioned his brother and sister-in-law, insisting that they knew something and were covering for Erik. They denied it. When agents pressed Sparre in an interrogation room at a nearby GBI office, he continued to deny killing the Swains. They kept pressing him—until he threw out a new idea.

He said he might know who committed the murders: his uncle Kenneth Metts. Metts was from the same maternal line as Erik and would have matched the hairs found in the hinge of the glasses by the bodies. He had also lived in Spring Bluff and was violent and racist. Conveniently for Sparre, his uncle was long dead.

Did he have a reason to think Metts killed the Swains? He said he didn't. No one had ever said anything about Metts confessing to the murders. Metts was twice the age of the killer as described by the church witnesses, and he had curly red hair. Sparre had no explanation for why, if his uncle did it, people said Sparre bragged about doing it himself. He still insisted that he hadn't admitted to the Swains' murders, though he had admitted to me—on tape—that he told Emily Head's family he'd killed the Swains. He said he was lying, trying to scare her.

The agents weren't moved by the Uncle Kenneth idea. But Sparre made it through the interrogation without incriminating himself further. The agents were disappointed to let him go again.

THE MORNING OF NOVEMBER 18, 2020. RISING DAUGHTER BAPTIST Church, Spring Bluff, Georgia.

The gravedigger's pickup creaked as its winch lifted a casket from the South Georgia dirt. Exhaust spewed from the tailpipe, floating through the graveyard next to Rising Daughter Baptist Church. The GBI was exhuming the body of Harold Swain.

Agents had gone to the Swains' remaining local relatives to ask for permission. The hope was that the killer's DNA could still be under Harold Swain's fingernails. Even forty years removed from the murder, a good sample could identify the killer—and not just his maternal line. Back in 1985, the crime lab didn't scrape under fingernails for testing, but exhuming Harold's body gave them one last chance. Agents from the task force stood quietly watching as a crime lab employee pried open the casket and assessed the remains. Slowly she began removing fingernails. She wrapped them in paper towels and passed them to an agent who secured them in tiny manila envelopes.

Once the agents concluded their search, the gravediggers closed the casket. The winch lowered it back in the ground, and the men covered it with dirt again.

23

Endings

One year after Dennis Perry's release, he wore a pinstriped suit with a fresh haircut to court for the moment he'd longed for: The DA was dropping all charges against him. DA Keith Higgins, who had trounced Jackie Johnson in the November 2020 election, shuffled into the courtroom and shook Perry's hand. The room went silent as Higgins stepped to the lectern.

"As a prosecutor, I have an obligation to seek and do justice, and sometimes that means righting a wrong," said Higgins. "This is one of those cases."

Higgins had reviewed evidence, talked with relatives of the Swains, and consulted with three leading members of the GBI task force. The evidence implicated Sparre, not Perry. The search for DNA under Harold Swain's fingernails hadn't yielded enough to test, and Sparre hadn't been charged. But Higgins said he had asked the Swains' family for their opinion, and they agreed that Perry should be exonerated. Higgins, who'd been the reform candidate, did not chastise, or even mention, the police and prosecutors who had sent Perry away for life with sloppy and illegal methods. He did not apologize for what his office did to Perry and the Swains' loved ones.

"I'm asking the court to grant this motion in the interest of justice," Higgins said.

The judge signed Perry's exoneration.

In a brief statement to the court, Perry looked the judge in the eye and said, with conviction, "Now that the justice system isn't focused on the wrong man, I hope there will be justice for Mr. and Mrs. Swain. I pray every day for justice for Harold and Thelma Swain."

When he was done, the gallery rang with applause. Perry walked arm in arm down the stairs with Brenda and his attorney Jennifer Whitfield. On the courthouse steps, Perry found Butch Kennedy. They had never met, had just seen each other once twenty years earlier during Perry's trial.

They embraced. Kennedy clutched Perry's hand as they cried together. Perry thanked Kennedy for all he'd done for him.

"Wish I could've done more," Kennedy said.

Perry already knew. Kennedy wanted Sparre prosecuted, but Perry's exoneration was the most profound validation Kennedy had experienced. He and Joe Gregory determined Perry was innocent in 1988, and now the system finally agreed. Perry knew that Kennedy's support—the affidavits he'd taken the time to write, the painful hours the terribly shy man spent being interviewed by *Undisclosed*, the memories he'd dredged up to support my investigation—was key to the effort to free Perry.

"Thank you," Perry said again as Kennedy released Perry's arm. They knew they were living through an epic story and felt they had triumphed at the end. They laughed, amazed.

Perry walked to the top of the courthouse steps and announced that he had a statement to read. Reporters extended microphones.

For more than twenty years, Perry hadn't been able to speak publicly about his case with honesty, for fear of offending the authorities whose help he needed. At last, Perry had no reason to care what
anyone thought.

Perry listed what he'd lost: "My freedom, my family, my health, my
house and my pets," he read, tears turning to anger. "My business I was
building, based on honesty and integrity and my word. It was all taken
from me.... The possibility of having my own children and watching
them grow." He read through the facts: He'd been cleared in 1988 only
to learn he was the only suspect the police focused on a decade later;
the prosecution was based on the word of a person with serious mental
issues who was paid $12,000 to testify.

"I lost my grandmother—my best friend. I lost her in 2014. I
lost my mother in 2017 and my father in 2020," Perry said, starting
to struggle. "I was never able to say goodbye or properly grieve them.
Having emotions is something you're robbed of in prison.... At this
time in my life, I should be able to have my finances in order so that
my wife and I can think about retirement. Instead, I have no income,
my health is no good, and I must start all over again. My wife works
hard," Perry said putting his arm around Brenda, "and has supported
me for twelve years. We should be able to retire together, but that's not
possible because of my wrongful conviction.

"Mom, Dad, Nanny," he said, turning his face to the blue sky,
squinting into the sun, "I love you and thank you for your belief in me."

When Perry finished, Kennedy turned, padded down the side-
walk toward the parking lot, hands in his pockets. In a moment he was
gone. On the steps, a TV reporter thrust forth a microphone. *What's
next for you, Mr. Perry?*

"Today," Perry said, pacing slightly in the shade of the courthouse
roof. He beamed—a day free was a miracle to Perry, even if he was just

walking around the yard or chasing his granddaughter around. And then, the reporter wanted to know, what was next for Perry *after* today?

"Tomorrow."

MIKE ELLERSON WAS THRILLED BY PERRY'S EXONERATION. BUT he was still waiting for justice for the Swains. We sat in his office at the College of Coastal Georgia police department while the Ahmaud Arbery murder trial played live on his computer. We talked a long time about his role in the church murders case and how he was frozen out when he said Perry was innocent.

After a while, Ellerson looked at the clock and noticed the end of his shift had arrived. He unclipped the badge from his shirt and started to loosen his collar.

"Don't mind me," Ellerson said, "I never wear a uniform home. Timeeeeeessss," he emphasized comically, "have changed. People don't like the police that much anymore now. So I don't move and do things the way I used to. I'm not cocky anymore."

As uncomfortable as the job could be amid widespread criticism of police, Ellerson welcomed change. We'd been watching it on his computer. Ellerson had worked alongside one of Arbery's killers in the same courthouses for years. He'd also worked with ex-DA Jackie Johnson, who now faced an indictment for her alleged mishandling of Arbery's case. And mighty Sheriff Smith had lost a comeback attempt in the 2012 election. An era had ended, Ellerson thought—thank God.

IN LATE 2021, I WAS STILL INVESTIGATING THE CASE WHEN I HAD time between other stories at the newspaper. I stayed in touch with Butch Kennedy and Joe Gregory, who believed that Sparre committed the murders but couldn't shake the thought that Donnie Barrentine was somehow involved. So far, my investigation had yielded no more evidence of Barrentine's involvement than theirs. His story had been that he and a friend did it, that Barrentine had waited outside as the friend pulled the trigger. Jeff Kittrell, the fellow gang member who first mentioned Barrentine to police, said he didn't know who the friend was. He thought he had blond hair, which wouldn't match brown-haired Sparre, though it isn't clear where Kittrell got the blond detail. Kennedy and Gregory had plenty of theories about who the man with Barrentine could've been. They wondered if the accomplice was connected to the rural enclave in Brantley County where Barrentine's drug gang was based. They didn't realize that another of their suspects had spent a lot of time in that tiny neighborhood: Erik Sparre. Sparre had family property there and lived there on and off, according to public records and my interviews. In 1990, he was charged with growing marijuana there by the GBI. Decades later, Sparre built his little green, barn-style house there— the one the GBI searched for evidence in the church murders. Sparre's house was less than a mile from Greg Barrentine's old home.

The original story about Barrentine and his "cold-blooded" friend was that they went to Rising Daughter Baptist to put pressure on the Swains' drug-trafficking relative, Lawrence Brown. Brown died in a car wreck in 2014. His stepdaughter, LaFane, who was raised by the Swains, declined to speak with me through relatives. In late 2019, I went to see Brown's wife, Theresa, at her home outside Savannah.

She was in a hospital bed in the living room with tubes coming from her nose. Theresa had suffered respiratory and other damage in the Thiokol ammunition factory explosion in Camden County decades earlier. Beneath the hum and hiss of her medical devices, I heard her weakened voice say that she didn't know of any involvement by her late husband. But she heard the rumors that the murders could've had something to do with him.

There's a lot of gossip, Brown told Theresa after the murders. *They're talking about I took Uncle Harold's money, saying that I killed Uncle Harold and Aunt Thelma.*

People thought that Brown had the Swains killed—with help from a white gunman—so he could collect their life insurance money. Indeed, shortly before the murders, he'd asked Harold Swain for money and been rebuffed. After the Swains' funeral, witnesses said Brown insisted that LaFane get the insurance money, and she later did. Brown told his wife he had nothing to do with the murders.

I believe you, Theresa said she told her husband, adding: *I don't want to talk about this ever again.*

AS AN INVESTIGATIVE JOURNALIST, I LEARNED EARLY ON THAT some of the best reporting takes place when you're sifting through the reporting you've already done. You can't read a document just once or review your interviews just once. There's far too much to value in rereading the documents, relistening to the tape once you're deeper in the investigation. Things that made no sense initially suddenly spring with meaning. Things you thought you understood become more complicated. Things you hadn't considered come to mind. In reviewing the evidence in the Swains' murders, all these things happened.

Listening back to my interview with Theresa, I realized I'd missed something initially. She said the "rumors flying around" said her husband was *involved* in the Swains' murders. That wasn't the story the detectives heard. Donnie Barrentine supposedly said that he went with a friend to Rising Daughter Baptist Church to "send a message" to Brown because Brown had run afoul of gang leaders and was hiding out. But was he really hiding? Cynthia Clayton told me that Lawrence and Theresa joined other relatives in Spring Bluff in the hours after the Swains were murdered. Brown even went to Rising Daughter while the police were investigating. Perhaps he felt safer with all the police and other people around. Harold Swain's late cousin, Nolan Frazier, told police that Brown was recently upset when Harold declined to loan him money. Frazier also said that Brown was aggressive when telling everyone that his stepdaughter, who'd been adopted by the Swains, was the sole beneficiary.

Before my stories published in the *AJC*, I had no evidence that Sparre and Barrentine had ever known each other. They both said they didn't. Other former drug traffickers who did business with the Barrentines told me they had never heard of Sparre. I didn't always find them credible. But then I spoke with a person who did seem credible. Asking to remain anonymous due to fear, they told me that Sparre hung around Barrentine's gang, socializing with members at dog and chicken fights and at the Satilla River. My source said that everyone in the area, including Sparre, knew what the Barrentines were doing in Brantley County, and everyone knew Greg Barrentine, who ran the local branch of the so-called Dixie Mafia. Back in 1985, the rumor around Brantley County was that Greg Barrentine was behind the murders at Rising Daughter and that Sparre had been the triggerman, though a motive wasn't clear.

"Erik," my source said, "would have done whatever Greg said to do."

Joe Gregory told me that one of his old confidential informants had been in touch after my stories appeared to say that Sparre and Donnie Barrentine knew each other. There was also this: One of the GBI's witnesses told them that Sparre had bragged about being involved with drug trafficking. "He was talking about planes, drugs, that he was in the Mafia."

As all of this swirled in my mind, I let myself wonder: Is it possible that Donnie Barrentine claimed that the murders were supposed to send a message to Brown to cover for the fact that Brown set the whole thing up for the insurance money? Barrentine only brought up

Brown after he knew the cops had heard about his drunken confession at the party.

I considered the insurance money another theory to explain the murders, a theory evidently weighed from the beginning by people who knew the Swains and Brown. Another theory raised to me was that Sparre was angry at Harold Swain because Swain cooperated with the authorities when Sparre allegedly attacked a customer at Choo Choo BBQ. Some people who knew Sparre thought he could have killed the Swains because of his alleged white supremacist views and Harold Swain's leadership in the African American community.

Whatever the motive was, I don't think this crime happened the way it was supposed to. Harold Swain surprised the gunman when he refused to speak with him outside, and then again when he fought back. Thelma Swain surprised the gunman by running to her husband's aid. How did the killer leave so many witnesses alive? He hadn't expected there to be any—he was going to confront Harold Swain outside. Maybe a partner was waiting to help deal with Swain but never got the chance.

Much more information on the motives could be contained in the records from the GBI's renewed investigation; the files aren't public record because the case remains open. The task force finished its investigation and turned all records over to the Brunswick District Attorney's Office in mid-2021, and prosecutors said they would review the evidence while considering charges for Sparre.

THE DENNY'S DINING ROOM WAS DIM ONE SATURDAY MORNING as I waited for Dennis and Brenda Perry. Dennis leaned on a hooked cane as he walked toward the table with his wife. He had been in physical therapy for several pinched nerves and neck issues, consequences of his construction career and the poor medical care in prison. Brenda Perry had a detached retina and recently found out she had glaucoma. Both of them hurt.

Have you seen the paper? Brenda asked me. *The Tribune & Georgian* had a new investigation out on the Camden County Sheriff's Office with the headline: "Get Out of Jail Free Card?" They laughed at how some things never change around here.

Brenda pulled out her phone to show me a before-and-after of Dennis on the day of his release and one year later. I could barely believe the face in the first photo, taken of Dennis smiling in his yard. His cheeks looked painted on bone. He was terribly pale. In the second photo, Dennis stood in the kitchen, dressed up for a night out: plaid button-down shirt, jeans, boots. He smiled broader and had put on weight. He glowed.

I don't even remember you looking like that, I said to Dennis. *I remember you looking great.*

GEORGIA HAS AN ARCANE PROCESS TO COMPENSATE PEOPLE who've been wrongfully convicted. They must win the ear of a state lawmaker who's willing to sponsor a resolution to pay them with state dollars. But Perry, unlike some others, had no trouble finding a sponsor because of the media attention and the GBI's renewed investigation. Four Republican and two Democratic lawmakers put forth a bill in January 2022 that would pay Perry $1.4 million. Lawmakers unanimously approved the bill. It was bittersweet for Perry because he knew that so many exonerees get nothing, and many become homeless.

Perry thought of what the money could do, and he started to cry. He wanted to buy his wife a new house. "Coming to see me for thirteen years, I know it took a lot of toll on her," he said. "I just want her to have something she can call hers, that we can call ours."

When he got the money, he bought a piece of land with a spacious home and a big yard down the road from their old place. It's an easy drive from Spring Bluff. It comforted Perry to be close to where he'd grown up, where he'd fished in the Little Satilla River with his grand-mother and his mom. Now when Perry visited the Satilla, he thought of all the people he'd lost. He turned his head to the sky, praying that those who were gone could hear him, that they were OK, that they knew he was OK now, that they knew how badly he still wanted jus-tice. When he looked into the dark water, Dennis saw his reflection, and all around him was the spreading sky.

ONE DAY NOT LONG AGO. RISING DAUGHTER MISSIONARY BAPTIST *Church, Spring Bluff, Georgia.*

A weary-looking man walked past three wooden crosses, each draped in a violet sash. Sunlight bounded off the stained glass windows, and the sun filtered through the canopy of massive oaks and pines. The church was closed, but Reverend Michael Rivers happened to be there. He walked across the yard to meet the man, who said he just needed someone to pray for him.

Rivers took his hand and began as they both closed their eyes.

"God, you say iron sharpens iron," Rivers prayed.

This was the promise of a church like Rising Daughter. It had been started as a refuge for people whose families escaped the horrors of slavery only to have their struggles redesigned, not ended, and through the years, it served anyone who needed help. People who weren't members, weren't Spring Bluff residents would stop by and ask for food or money or prayer or a recommendation for a job. People stopped by because, especially if they're from South Georgia, they're taught—or learn—that a church is where you can go when you can't go anywhere else.

You can never go so far that you can't be forgiven, the Apostle Paul revealed in the last passages Harold Swain saw before he was murdered. If any person could be saved, any person had to be welcomed. It hadn't changed since the Swains were killed by a man taking advantage of the church's openness.

You still could walk down this lonesome highway hurting in a bad way and feel the preacher take your hand in the churchyard.

"I'm standing on your promises, Father," Rivers prayed, "that you will supply every need."

Epilogue

In late November 2024, after a long delay in reviewing the evidence, a prosecutor contacted the GBI to say that the DA's office had decided to prosecute Erik Sparre. GBI agents put together a plan to arrest him.

Sparre had gone quietly about his life at his rural home, wondering about his fate while living a changed life. He'd become a pariah in his community as decades of allegations of racism, threats of violence, and domestic abuse became public knowledge through widespread media coverage. He was investigated in his mother's death, though the GBI eventually said that the evidence didn't support ruling it a homicide, calling it an accidental asphyxiation, apparently from losing oxygen when the bag covered her face. The GBI had tapped his phone and listened to his calls. He knew that because he—and every person he spoke to on that phone—received a letter acknowledging, as legally required, that their communications had been intercepted.

On December 9, the sixty-one-year-old saw police at the door, and he must've known what they wanted: him. He surrendered peacefully and was booked into the Camden County jail on two counts of aggravated assault and two counts of murder in the deaths of Harold and Thelma Swain. He was denied bond. It was four months shy of the forty-year anniversary of the murders.

The news brought a collective sigh of relief to many—people who had known the Swains, Spring Bluff residents, members of the Camden County NAACP, police, and lawyers who'd investigated the case. They had feared the chance for accountability had slipped away and were overjoyed to learn that it hadn't.

Pearl J. Cole, one of Harold Swain's three surviving siblings, praised the arrest on Facebook. "Justice was done yesterday," Cole, a minister, wrote. She'd watched two and a half years earlier when Perry was exonerated in court—a profoundly complex thing for a family to process after authorities assured them two decades earlier that they had the right man.

"Don't stop praying; he will hear your cry. He didn't let us down," Cole wrote.

Charlie Swain could hardly believe it when he heard the news. "I'm very glad they have the right person now," he told me, recalling with a chill how the state tried to send Perry, an innocent man, to death row. He said he was grateful for everyone who worked on the investigation through the years. He just wished more people were alive to see this.

Emily Head Drury, Sparre's first ex-wife, who reported his taped confession in 1986, died fearing that justice for the Swains—and for Sparre—would never come. One of her two sons with Sparre, Kalem Head, told me that he always suspected that Sparre could've been involved in his mother's 2013 murder. Sparre told me that he was innocent and that he was investigated and cleared by the police. It brought little comfort to Kalem's family in 2018 when a state prisoner was indicted in her murder after officials said they found his DNA under Drury's fingernail—with no other evidence. A prosecutor told me there was no proof the DNA got under her fingernail during the murder and that the crime didn't match the patterns in the convicted serial rapist's other known crimes. Kalem said he didn't think that man did it; he still wondered if Sparre did. He said some of his family had feared that Sparre would come after them, until his arrest in the Swains' murders brought them peace of mind.

I asked Kalem what his mom—the woman whose statements to police made Sparre a suspect in the church murders in the first place—would think of his arrest. "She would probably say that God and karma finally caught up to him," Kalem said, "and that he is getting what he deserves."

What did Kalem think? "In my eyes, if he has to spend the rest of his life in prison, that's great," he said, "but he's getting off easy."

No one could reach Butch Kennedy to give him the news. Kennedy, seventy-nine, had suffered a couple of strokes and grown more forgetful. After hearing nothing all night, Dennis Perry decided to drive over to the old detective's house. Perry had kept in touch with Kennedy. They had both been praying for justice for the Swains.

Perry heard a TV blaring and a dog barking, but he pounded on the door for five minutes without hearing any sign of Kennedy. He was about to get worried when a groggy Kennedy opened the door and greeted him. Kennedy stepped out into the yard and leaned against his truck.

You might want to sit down, buddy, Perry said, and Kennedy did.

They arrested Erik Sparre, Perry said.

Kennedy immediately began to sob. He hugged Perry, his tears dampening Perry's shoulder. Kennedy cried and cried until he finally had something to say.

I can go on and pass away now, he said. *All I wanted was to see you go free and to see this day.*

ACKNOWLEDGMENTS

This book exists thanks to the work of untold numbers of people who in one way or another contributed to finding answers on the murders of Harold and Thelma Swain. The case was examined by police, attorneys, the Swains' relatives, the Georgia Innocence Project and its corporate pro bono partners, interns, office workers, reporters, podcasters. I can't name all the helpers simply because no one knows all their names. If you think there's any chance this could refer to you, it does. Thank you.

I thank every person, named in these pages or not, who spoke with me for their contributions. To everyone who declined, I respect your decision.

The book also exists thanks to the many others who helped me along the way, especially Jane Dystel, my brilliant agent, and her colleagues at Dystel Goderich & Bourret LLC, who believed in me and this book. Drew Elizabeth Weitman brought the book to W. W. Norton and proceeded to give me absolutely stellar editing, spot-on feedback, and made me feel like the book was important to her personally. I owe an unimaginable debt to Caroline Adams, who came in to edit when Drew left Norton for other opportunities and who made the final product so much better with repeated great ideas. At *The Atlanta Journal-Constitution*, top editors, including Shawn McIntosh and Kevin Riley, sanctioned my reporting and became champions for my work. My first editor on this investigation and project was Jan Winburn, who I would take a bullet for and taught me so much. My direct editor Shannon McCaffery put up with my obsession over this investigation and did what all great editors do: When one of your people is on to something big and important, let them go after it. A later editor, Jennifer Brett, was also patient with me, understanding the gravity. She also convinced higher-ups that this story deserved more space than most, leading to my original investigative story, "The Imperfect Alibi," being printed in a special section in the paper—something that was common in years past but all but unheard of at the time. It took a small army of people across the newspaper to bring the story to the world, and I'm grateful for each and every one of them. Susan Hogan and Bill Rankin contributed editing to that story, and Hogan helped with her keen eye on subsequent stories. The paper's visual editor Sandra Brown came up with the name "The Imperfect Alibi." The visual department did a stellar job, capturing remarkable scenes that were featured in the acclaimed documentary the paper released, titled "The Imperfect Alibi." Filmmakers Ryon and Tyson Horne, with help from photojournalist Hyosub Shin, produced a film that is powerful, intimate, chilling, and satisfying.

Hannah Riley, the then-spokesperson for the Georgia Innocence Project, had the idea to ask if I'd like to report on one of the nonprofit's cases in 2019, leading to this investigation. Susan Simpson of *Undisclosed* shared records, tips, and invaluable advice and encouragement.

Without the Knight-Wallace Fellowship at the Wallace House Center for Journalists, this book would have taken ten years longer. To the other fellows, thank you for your support, friendship, and for inspiring me: Elizabeth Aguilera, Roberson Alphonse, Rustin Dodd, Sharif Hassan, Peter Hoffman, Yunhee Kim, Mila Koumpilova, Efrat Lachter, Victor Kai Shing Law, Jaime Lowe, Iuliia Mendel, Kwan Ling Mok, Josh Raab, Tamanna Rahman, 'Fisayo Soyombo, Ben Steverman, Doris Truong. I owe a debt to the Logan Nonfiction Program and the fellows, who gave early feedback: Alice Driver, Karen Pinchin, Viv Li, Paige Bethmann, Pedro de Filippis, Max Duncan, Marjolaine Grappe, Megan Kimble, Alissa Quart, Angela Saini, Justine van der Leun.

I'm profoundly grateful to my early readers who gave tremendously helpful feedback: Josie Duffy Rice, Johnny Kauffman, Mila Koumpilova, Jerad Walker, Bronwen Dickey, and Fatemeh Jamalpour. For their support and caring, I thank my family—those living and those gone. And to my friends for their support and inspiration: Thomas Lake, Lisa Pollak, Shaun Raviv, Charles McNair, Janel Davis, Tyler Estep, Melissa Hall, Lynette Clemetson, Ashley Bates, Max Blau, Greg Bluestein, Sonam Vashi, Jesse Herrin and family, Hafizah Geter, Tyler Hayes and family, Byron Ferguson, Brian Goldstone, Terry Dickson, Ben Montgomery, Thomas Mullen, Kyle Daniel and family, the Lake family, the Stewart family, Drew DuBose and family, Sonia Paul, Sharif Youssef, Raheem Hosseini, Jeremy Collins, Tommy Tomlinson, Susie Nielson, Melissa Segura, the Screenhouse Crew, the SSI Crew, the unfortunately named Sharpeshooters Atlanta Writers Crew, and many others, including Linda Gregerson and Steven Mullaney.

NOTES ON SOURCES

The reporting for this book included reading nearly fifteen thousand pages of police and court records, conducting interviews with over one hundred people, listening to the twenty-four-hour-plus *Undisclosed* season on Dennis Perry's case, searching for old records in back rooms at various courthouses, reviewing hundreds of newspaper articles and various videos, making many public records requests, and much more.

All discussion in the book about police procedure and the wisdom in those procedures is informed by my study in the Michigan Innocence Clinic, where I investigated potential wrongful convictions and researched their causes. This work was unpaid as part of the Knight-Wallace Fellowship at the University of Michigan. I also took the Innocence Clinic course on wrongful convictions, taught by Dave Moran, Imran Syed and Elizabeth Cole. I read numerous scientific studies on the tactics and interviewed experts.

In cases where I reference the source of information in the text of the book, I won't repeat it here except to add more context. This includes scenes that involve me, such as all the interviews I describe conducting. Details of all scenes that include me come from my notes, audio recordings of interviews, promptly memorialized observations, and photographs.

Former sheriff Bill Smith declined to speak with me for my investigation. As with everyone else, I did my best to present Smith's previously articulated positions on any matters of potential contention clearly. No one is required to speak with me, and I respect that completely.

PROLOGUE

The age of the church comes from Camden County property records, which list its date of construction as 1900. In my experience with property records of that age in South Georgia, they can sometimes be less than precise due to the then-nascent notion that construction must be registered with the local government. Because of this, it is possible, or even likely, that the church, and certainly the idea to build it, rose before 1900. The name Rising Daughter Baptist Church is used here and throughout the book because it was the name for generations until, in the years after the murders, the name was changed to Rising Daughter Missionary Baptist Church. My understanding is that many people called it Rising Daughter for short, but because I am not from Spring Bluff or a member or the church, I chose a standard shorthand in hopes that it would be more respectful than an outsider using an inside term. After the church changed its name, the new name is used in the book: Rising Daughter Missionary Baptist Church. Descriptions of the church and life there come from interviews—some conducted and memorialized by police, some by me—of current and former church members.

Robert Cummings, the longtime head of the Camden County NAACP, told me about the group holding meetings at Rising Daughter and other local churches, just as other civil rights groups, including the Rev. Martin Luther King Jr.'s Southern Christian Leadership Conference, had. Moving the meeting location frequently meant that those who might wish harm to civil rights activists would have to work harder to find them, as the Center for American Progress noted in the June 9, 2004, article "The Role of Religion in the Civil Rights Movements." The history is now so well-known and deep that the state of Georgia's tourism office promotes historic African American churches as destinations for people looking to learn more about the civil rights movement.

Information about employment patterns in the county comes from interviews with numerous residents and writings and books collected by the Bryan-Lang Archives, the county's history library, whose staffers were very helpful. These include *Camden's Challenge: A History of Camden County, Georgia*, by Marguerite Reddick, with a number of contributors to the tome first published in 1976 and updated in 2004, and James T. Vocelle's 1913 book *Reminiscences of old St. Marys*. In weighing the power of Gilman Paper Company, I consulted "Democracy and the Good Life in a Company Town," published in *Harper's* in 1972 and written by Harrison Wellford and Peter Schuck, associates of researcher Ralph Nader. I watched Mike Wallace's 1972 *60 Minutes* report on St. Marys to learn more still about the grip Gilman had on the community. I referred to "Owing Your Soul to the Company Store," Ralph Nader and Mark Green's 1973 *New York Review of Books* exposé on businesses that ran pockets of the United States, including Gilman Paper Company in St. Marys. James Fallows's 2014 article in *The Atlantic*, "The Transformation of a Company Town: St. Marys," was helpful in tracking the city's transformation through the years, including on how the prominence of the Kings' Bay naval submarine base's helped diminish the paper company's influence.

To find out how residents and officials thought about Gilman's and the naval base, I used information from interviews and read decades of newspaper articles from *The Brunswick News*, *The Tribune & Georgian*, *The Atlanta Journal-Constitution*, and others. These sources informed my descriptions of the ways in which the community was affected by both Gilman's long era of overwhelming dominance and the changes brought to Camden County by the naval base. I studied US Census data to describe demographics.

Information about Cumberland Island comes from archived newspaper articles, including from *The Atlanta Journal-Constitution*.

My descriptions of life in Spring Bluff in 1985 come from interviews with numerous former and current residents and archival photographs. Because multiple people buried in the historic Black cemetery were born before the end of the Civil War, it is safe to assume they had been born into slavery because the region is known to have had few free Black people and far more enslaved Africans than white people.

Harold Swain's birthplace comes from his obituary. Details about his fishing are from interviews with people who knew him.

My description of how the investigation had unfolded comes from the case file, numerous interviews with witnesses, and investigators who worked the case.

PART I: WAVES

Descriptions of the tide and wildlife in the marshes come from personal observation as well as information from the University of Georgia Marine Extension and Georgia Sea Grant.

1. THE MAN IN THE VESTIBULE

In telling the story of Harold and Thelma's last moments and the immediate aftermath, I relied on transcripts of audio-recorded police interviews with each of the church witnesses who spoke with detectives within hours, as well as two other police witness interviews.

The visual description of how the outside of the church, as well as the inside, looked comes from photographs police took that night.

The detail about the moon comes from data stored by the Astronomical Applications Department of the US Naval Observatory.

Biographical information about Harold and Thelma Swain comes from my interviews with relatives, people who knew them, their obituaries, and US Census records.

Details about the church witnesses come from their interviews with police and with WJXT, the Jacksonville, Florida, news station.

2. THE OFFICER'S DUTY

The details of Butch Kennedy's arrival at the scene, his actions, his dress, his thoughts and observations there are from many interviews with Kennedy, as well as police records. His biographical details come from interviews with him, people who'd worked with him, others who knew him, and newspaper articles. The date he became a police officer is from his file with the Georgia Peace Officer Standards and Training Council.

The county's low level of crime is supported by interviews with local police, officials, and residents, as well as archived newspaper articles on crime.

All dialogue quoted in this chapter is from transcripts of recorded police interviews.

I learned how the news of the murders spread and about the scene in the churchyard through interviews with the Swains' relatives and loved ones, as well as from Kennedy and Joe Gregory.

The owner of Reed's Package told the *Undisclosed* podcast that the scene at the church was eerily quiet before they looked in the vestibule.

Police records and interviews with Gregory were used to explain his role as a GBI agent, how he was summoned to the scene, what he found there, how he felt, what he thought, and what he did. Biographical details about Gregory come from interviews with him, his wife, Pat Gregory, and people who've worked with him.

Information about DNA testing's history and historical use in criminal cases comes from interviews with DNA testing experts and scientific papers, including the 2004 Baylor University article by Rana Saad, "Discovery, Development, and Current Applications of DNA Identity Testing."

Details about the physical condition of the scene and physical evidence come from crime scene photos and records in the homicide investigation case file.

Thomas Baker's status as a plaintiff, as well as the fact that the county had no high school for African American students until 1952, is from an Associated Press article that ran in May 16, 1985 edition of The Brunswick News under the headline "Camden County won't switch to district election setup."

Local historian Tara D. Fields's meticulously researched 2006 article "Murder at Boggy Swamp Plantation" explains what locals called "The Gallows."

Slaveholders and their plantations were lauded in local history books.

Discussion about the state of racial relations and how people thought about them comes from interviews with numerous residents and newspaper articles chronicling incidents of various fights along racial lines. Kennedy and Gregory's thoughts about the possible motives come from interviews with them and records they made in the case file.

Interlude: The details about Harold Swain's work and presence at Choo Choo BBQ, as well as the restaurant's reputation, come from interviews with relatives, people who knew him, and those who just observed him at the store. The giant golf ball at EPCOT opened in 1982, according to lostepcot.com.

3. THE KILLER'S FACE

Kennedy told me how he felt and what he thought when he woke up on the morning after the murders. He told me what he wore and drove.

Cora Fisher's interview comes from the transcript made from the audio recording and from interviews with Kennedy. Details about Fisher come from people who knew her, from *Undisclosed*, and from her obituary.

Details of Gregory's life, trouble adjusting to the culture in South Georgia, and his relationship with wife Pat come from interviews with both and from their son Tommy Gregory.

The Brunswick hospital's renovation was discussed in numerous articles in *The Brunswick News*.

Details from the autopsies come from autopsy reports the doctor created for Harold Swain and Thelma Swain and from photographs. Gregory also told me about the experience.

Loved ones gave me the details used about the grief and the Swains' home after the murders.

Information about the Swains' daughter and her adoption come from police records and court records.

All witness interviews in this chapter come from transcripts of the audio-recorded conversations and from police reports.

The TV news segment comes from the archived footage.

The Identi-Kit scene is from police reports and a transcript of the interview.

For the discussion on police sketches and the trouble with them as well as with eyewitness identification in general, I consulted numerous academic studies, articles, and reports, including: D. Michael Risinger and Lesley C. Risinger, "Innocence Is Different: Taking Innocence into Account Reforming Criminal Procedure," in the January 2012 edition of *The New York Law School Law Review*; "Reevaluating Lineups: Why Witnesses Make Mistakes and How to Reduce the Chance of Misidentification," a report of the Benjamin N. Cardozo School of Law at Yeshiva University in New York City through a partnership with the national nonprofit Innocent Project; the 2003 book *Actual Innocence: When Justice Goes Wrong and How to Make it Right*, by Barry Scheck, Peter Neufeld, and Jim Dwyer; and "Not Photographs: The Misunderstood Police Composite Sketch," by Jennifer Vogel and Madeleine Baran, a helpful primer on sketches published by *APM Reports* on September 20, 2016. I also consulted the 1997 *Frontline* episode "What Jennifer Saw."

Kennedy told me what he thought about Cora Fisher's sketch, that Gwendolyn Owens didn't approve of the final composite, and about the discussions around the composite. Owens politely declined to speak with me.

4. A CROSS FOR EVERYONE

Cynthia Clayton told me about her relationship with her aunt and uncle, Harold and Thelma Swain, as well as about their last days and their funeral. Other loved ones and residents described the funeral to me, including Harold Swain's cousin and longtime employee Joe Frazier and the Swains' goddaughter Eloise Baker.

In addition to interviews, the weather is described with newspaper archives.

I also used the funeral programs provided by the funeral home.

Joe Frazier, who was one of many who remembered Harold Swain's love of baseball, told me about Swain going to the World Series. Robert Cummings, the then-head of the county NAACP, told me about Harold Swain's affiliation and work in the community. Artie Jones Jr., the county's first Black elected official, also told me about Swain's efforts.

I consulted US Census records for details on the Swains' early years.

Cynthia Clayton and her mother, Earnestine, who is Thelma Swain's sister, told me about her and what she did for the family.

I've been to the Swains' graves multiple times.

Details about the tips to police come from police records.

Kennedy and Gregory told me about the process and how it felt.

The news conference was written about in *The Brunswick News*' March 26, 1985, edition.

For the impact of the mystery on the community, I used information from Spring Bluff residents and Rising Daughter members, as well as newspaper articles, including the May 1985 article by Fred Hill in *The Southeast Georgian*, titled "Questions Still Haunt Spring Bluff Area."

Interlude: The scene with the deputies and their traffic stop comes from police reports.

5. CHANGING AND STAYING THE SAME

The biographical information and critics' thoughts on Sheriff Bill Smith come from numerous reports in area newspapers and files from the Georgia Bureau of Investigation.

Information about Sheriff Willie Smith comes from historic newspaper articles and interviews with people who knew him, including Robert Cummings, the head of the local NAACP, who pressed him to hire Black deputies. Cummings told me about his much better relationship with Bill Smith.

Information about Gilman Paper Company comes from interviews with many residents and the reports used in the prologue.

Details on Sheriff Bill Smith come from numerous interviews with people who worked for him and knew him, as well as GBI records that include audio-recorded interviews with Smith. Smith denied all wrongdoing.

Many newspaper articles were written about corrupt Georgia sheriffs in the 1980s, and the history, as well as rumors, spread so rampantly that even I heard them as a child.

To describe drug trafficking on Interstate 95, I read many newspaper articles from the time about the issue and interviewed former Camden County deputies.

The history of Ronald Reagan's seized asset program was documented in real time by news accounts and is memorialized on the websites of federal agencies, including the US Marshals Service. Many reports have addressed criticism that the program has lacked oversight, including the March 2017 report by US Department of Justice's Office of the Inspector General titled "Review of the Department's Oversight of Cash Seizure and Forfeiture Activities."

I learned how Sheriff Smith spent the money through GBI records, the sheriff's office bank records, and interviews with residents, former employees, and investigators.

Kennedy and Gregory told me about the trouble of having too many suspects because of the generic look of the composite sketch. They told me how they dealt with it, including by praying together.

6. THE SMUGGLER

Kennedy and Gregory told me about learning of and going to see Donnie Barrentine, and they memorialized details in reports. I used the transcript of the audio-recorded interviews they did at the Telfair County Jail. I learned about the gang through those interviews, as well as subsequent interviews that detectives conducted with others. I also interviewed people who knew or were associated with the gang, including Donnie Barrentine. Susan Simpson of *Undisclosed* did great reporting on the group.

I found out about the bullet holes in the ceiling from a man who later owned Greg Barrentine's house.

All interviews are from police reports and transcripts.

Interlude: Artie Jones told me this story, and I read newspaper accounts from the time.

7. THE RELATIVE

The details of the detectives' second visit to the Telfair County Jail come from interview transcripts, reports, and my interviews.

Lawrence Brown's backstory with Gilman Paper Company comes from court records and newspaper articles in *The Brunswick News*, *The Atlanta Journal-Constitution*, and others.

Details of Brown's drug arrest in 1985 are contained in federal law enforcement and court records first obtained and published by the *Undisclosed* podcast. I also spoke with Kennedy, Gregory, and Brown's wife, Theresa, about his time in federal custody and witness protection.

Kennedy told me about visiting Brown and Brown refusing to speak with him.

Barrentine's time card is in the case file. The detectives told me about checking his alibi, and I referred to their notes. Gregory told me that Barrentine had missed work the day after the murders.

Information about Vanzola Williams and the lineup featuring Barrentine comes from police records, court testimony, and Williams's statements on *Unsolved Mysteries* in the 1988 segment on the Swain murders.

Unsolved Mysteries included the detail about Barrentine telling the detectives that he in fact told the party he'd killed two Black people in a church but then claimed it was a lie. Barrentine has said he doesn't remember telling the detectives that he was lying when he spoke at the party. He also said he doesn't remember making the statement at the party, though multiple witnesses told investigators they remembered it.

Details about Foster's kinesic technique come from interviews with police who used it and from Foster's literature and public statements. The quotes attributed to Foster come from his statements in a video titled "D. Glenn Foster: The Kinesic Interview Technique (Insights #1)," which was uploaded to YouTube.

Kennedy and Gregory told me about what Foster said after interrogating Barrentine.

Barrentine's polygraph result is in the police case file.

In discussing dubious credibility of polygraphs, I read scientific studies, including "A Review of the Polygraph: History, Methodology and Current Status," published in 2015 by J. Synnott, D. Dietzel, and M. Ioannou in *Crime Psychology Review*. I also reviewed the U.S. Supreme Court decision barring polygraph results from being used as evidence in criminal proceedings in *United States v. Scheffer*.

Gregory testified to and told me about Barrentine's alleged statement about how he was "gonna fry."

Details about the arrest warrant process come from a copy of the warrant and interviews with Kennedy and Gregory. Information about criticism of DA Thomas comes from various newspaper articles and public grand jury presentments.

Gregory and Kennedy told me about Gregory's conversation with DA Thomas about the warrant (Thomas died more than a decade ago). Gregory has also sworn to the details in affidavits and court testimony.

Nolan Frazier's statements about Lawrence Brown are from police records.

8. "I'M THE MOTHER FUCKER"

The detectives told me how they reacted when Barrentine went to federal prison.

Details of Erik Sparre's alleged statements about killing the Swains and his treatment of Emily Head's family are from multiple police records memorializing the episode, including Head's interview. Sparre told me he is innocent. For allegedly threatening to kill Head's family while claiming responsibility for the Swains' murders, Sparre was indicted for terroristic threats. Court records say he pleaded out to simple battery in the case, which was worked by prosecutor John B. Johnson III.

Kennedy told me how he remembered Sparre from prior incidents, including when Kennedy arrested Sparre outside Choo Choo BBQ.

Kennedy didn't recall Sheriff Smith attending the interview, but Chad Head, Emily's brother, later testified that Smith was also there with Kennedy. Kennedy told me that Deputy Stan Edgy was there too.

Information about Emily Head leaving Sparre comes from her statements in police records and a copy of her divorce filing.

I interviewed various people about Fred Sparre and his views, including former coworkers, relatives, and others who knew or had encountered him. Fred's father's emigration from Denmark to Iowa is documented in US Census records.

Rhonda Tyson told me about the "Heil Odin" trend in the Sparre home. She also told me about Erik Sparre's alleged racist views, along with nearly every person I interviewed about him. Those people included former romantic partners, relatives, friends, and others who had interacted with him. Sparre told me he is not racist.

Kennedy noted Sparre's other arrest at Choo Choo BBQ in his application for a search warrant for Sparre's parents' home. The warrant and adjusted sketch are in the police case file.

Details of the search and Sparre's alibi come from police reports in the case file.

Gregory and Kennedy told me how they viewed the possibility of Sparre's guilt.

Interlude: Joe Frazier told me how the trauma and grief of witnessing the murders affected his late mother. He told me about growing up looking up to Harold Swain and about working with him. He told me about the cars.

9. UNSOLVED MYSTERY

All descriptions of the "Slain Swain" segment are gleaned from the show and police reports. The date it first aired is confirmed in police records and IMDb.

Kennedy and Gregory told me about their phone call about the glasses.

The detail about how many cases *Unsolved Mysteries* claimed to have solved comes from a May 28, 1988, article in *The Brunswick News* under the headline "Camden County Murders Subject of Upcoming 'Unsolved Mysteries.'"

The television viewership information comes from an Associated Press list published in the November 9, 1988, edition of *Lancaster New Era* (Pennsylvania).

The information on how shows like *Unsolved Mysteries* and *America's Most Wanted* brought viewers far deeper into pending investigations than police traditionally did comes from interviews with officials from the era, as well as a career spent reading newspaper clippings dating back decades about open criminal cases and observing that articles almost never included all key details and frequently included police declining to give more information. The reason for the culture of holding it close to the vest is mostly that investigators don't want their at-large perpetrators to know everything the cops know; police use this void of knowledge to try to figure out what unpublished details of the crime the suspect might know. It was, and continues to be, standard procedure for police around the world.

Cynthia Clayton told me about *Unsolved Mysteries* using the photo of Harold Swain's sister and calling her Thelma Swain, how she felt about the investigation at the time, and how she responded to Gregory's statement on the show that his initial guess that the killer was a "transient" could be correct. Gregory told me how he actually felt.

Clayton and Kennedy told me how police gave the Swains' loved ones fewer and fewer updates.

Information about the tips called into the show come from the phone bank tip log, which is in the police case file.

The former coworker testified during Dennis Perry's trial about what he told him when they saw the composite sketch in the newspaper. Perry told me about his relative mentioning the resemblance.

Kennedy and others told me what they knew about Brian "Corky" Rozier and about his reputation. Kennedy told me they found no evidence of Harold Swain finding any marijuana. Perry and Kennedy told me about Rozier's reputation. Rozier's widow told me he wouldn't have lied on Perry.

That Perry didn't wear glasses, do the type of work the killer was suspected to do, or have a car comes from court testimony, police interview records, and my interviews with Perry and people who knew him at the time in 1985.

Gregory has sworn to the details of his investigation into Perry, finding that he had a strong alibi, in affidavits and court testimony.

Nolan Frazier told police about his suspicions of Brown after the murders. Cynthia Clayton told me that some in the family had been suspicious of Brown too.

Kennedy told me about his frustration with figuring out the whole truth of the case.

The number of tips cleared after the show comes from police records.

Kennedy told me about drinking beer on the porch and how he felt.

PART II: IN DARKENED WATER

The description of the Satilla River's dark water and the cause of the color and the water's reflective properties comes from personal observation and articles on the phenomenon by various environmental and government organizations. A helpful primer is available on the website of the Ogeechee Riverkeeper, titled "Tannins and blackwater rivers," published on May 29, 2020.

10. ON THE PATH

Mike Ellerson told me about singing in class and his experience on the night of the murders. I also consulted public records and studied maps.

Ellerson told me about the argument he overheard between Sheriff Bill

Smith and Robert Cummings. Cummings told me about it, too, and confirmed that it was related to allegations of Black prisoners being beaten in the jail.

Ellerson told me about his jail tour.

Information on the raid is from the GBI case file from the investigation into Smith.

I knew about McIntosh County sheriff Tom Poppell's corruption from the stunning *Praying For Sheetrock*, by Melissa Fay Greene. I confirmed Poppell's relationship to Smith's girlfriend through obituaries.

I've seen prisoner work crews along roadsides across the South throughout my life and in courthouses as a journalist. I've reported on a trustee program and learned more through speaking with people who'd been on the crews. I've also read about the history of the phenomenon and its horrific roots in convict leasing in *Slavery by Another Name*, by David A. Blackmon.

Details on how Smith allegedly used prisoner labor come from the GBI case files from both times the agency investigated him.

I know about the temptation of giving in to labor exploitation of people behind bars from interviews with people who'd worked on the crews.

Details about Kennedy and Gregory's involvement in the investigation into the deputies are from the GBI case file of that inquiry. Kennedy and Gregory told me about the tensions the case caused because the deputies were close to top brass at the sheriff's office.

Information on the high-ranking deputies' indictment—the charges were ultimately dropped—comes from GBI records and news articles at the time.

I reviewed the lawsuit filed against the sheriff and read news articles about it.

I know about the sheriff's friend's interest in Confederate history through GBI records, including a report from when an agent called his house. Instead of saying hello when he answered, the sheriff's friend said, "Confederate Embassy."

Kennedy told me about his frustration with the Swains case still being unsolved. He also told me about the sheriff's frustration.

Kennedy told me about his departure from the sheriff's office and how he felt. Smith told *Undisclosed* that Kennedy decided to resign. Kennedy told me that the sheriff wanted him to resign, which he took as being fired. In hindsight, Kennedy thought that Smith listed it as a resignation to be nice because if he was fired, it would make it harder for Kennedy to get work in the future.

Gregory told me about his caseload.

Ellerson and Kennedy told me about working together and Ellerson's ascent at the sheriff's office.

Ellerson told me about wanting to take on the Swain case.

11. BATON

Everything about Kennedy's work at the tax commissioner's office, how he felt about things, and his life is from Kennedy and others who knew him back then.

The description of Gregory's efforts to get more evidence on Barrentine is from the case file and interviews with Gregory.

There is a GBI report of the interview where Gregory brought along Kennedy.

I learned about Smith's reputation and drug interdiction program through interviews with people who worked for him, knew him, and lived in Camden County, including Rich Gamble, the retired head of criminal investigations at the Kings Bay naval base who unsuccessfully ran against Smith in 2004 after years of questioning the actions of a man he'd always been friendly with. I also read numerous articles in *The Brunswick News* and investigative reporting on Smith's administration in *The Tribune & Georgian* and *The Florida Times-Union*.

John Edwards, a retired GBI special agent in charge who twice investigated Sheriff Smith, told me about the concerns that Smith wouldn't be convicted.

Gregory told me about the transition in his career, his car wreck and how it ended his career.

Ellerson told me about various cases he worked, and I read about them in newspaper articles. Ellerson told me about starting to work on the Swain case and his thoughts.

I heard about the rumor of Smith's potential challenger in the 2000 election from *Undisclosed* and then from others I spoke with.

I know about the migration of white conservatives from the Democratic Party to the Republican Party from living in the area at the time and covering politics at *The Cherokee Tribune* and from numerous interviews with veteran politicians through the years. I researched Camden County voting history.

Details of Dale Bundy's employment are from his personnel file and contract.

Ellerson told me his thoughts on having to assist Bundy.

Details on Bundy's career and work history are from his personnel file and court testimony.

Ellerson told me things about the case that were personal, and I read newspaper articles about the case as well as court records.

I learned that Bundy was from the McCarthy family from *Undisclosed*.

Information about homicide trends is from data held by the US Department of Justice.

I read various articles from the time about the phenomenon of cold case investigators, including an Associated Press story by Larry McShane, which appeared in the April 4, 1999, edition of *The Montana Standard* under the headline "Detectives Hot on the Trail of Cold Cases." That article is the source for the numbers of arrests around the country. I also researched cold cases and their limitations through the National Registry of Exonerations and at the Michigan Innocence Clinic.

I know about missing evidence from court testimony and interviews with Kennedy, Gregory, and Bundy.

Details on the first days of Bundy's investigation are from his investigative report and his interviews with Susan Simpson of *Undisclosed*.

Interlude: Ellerson told me about the experience at Sandy Myers's house after his murder and the details about tracking down and telling his brother to turn himself in. I also read newspaper articles and court records.

12. COLD SHOULDER DAY

Details about Bundy's approach of and interview with Cora Fisher come from Bundy's report, his *Undisclosed* interviews, and court testimony.

Details here about Fisher are from court testimony, her obituary, *Undisclosed*, and news articles.

I've experienced the weather and been to Jane Beaver's trailer.

Details about Beaver are from Bundy's statements, Beaver's testimony, her personnel file from the University of Georgia's outpost on Sapelo Island, her obituary, and interviews with people who knew her.

Details of Beaver's interview are from Bundy's report, statements, and testimony.

Court records, police records, and interviews that I conducted describe Perry's relationship with Beaver's daughter, as well as his life around that time.

Ellerson told me about the visit to Vanzola Williams's house. Bundy testified about it and spoke with *Undisclosed* about his decision to break protocol by showing Williams one man's photo instead of a group. Williams testified about the detectives' visit.

Ellerson told me about reading Perry's alibi documents in the case file and how he felt knowing that Perry was Bundy's focus. Bundy has said he never saw those documents.

Information about Bundy going to Perry's house is from court records, his report, interviews. and *Undisclosed*.

Ellerson told me about getting frozen out of the investigation after telling everyone at the meeting that Perry was innocent. Ellerson told me how he reacted.

The scene with Rhonda Minder comes from the case file and my interviews with her.

The interview with Perry's mom is from the case file, along with interviews with people who knew her.

The coatrack alibi information comes from the case file, *Undisclosed*, and interviews with Perry and Clayton Tomlinson. Donna Nash's interview is from the case file.

To tell about the arrest and subsequent interrogation, I used the case file and interviews with Perry and his attorney, Jennifer Whitfield.

13. FACING DEATH

Information about Kennedy and Gregory learning about the arrest and how they reacted is from interviews with them and Tommy Gregory.

Perry and his brother told me about the Bible gift. Perry showed it to me.

Perry told me about the experience in jail and how he felt.

The descriptions of the lives of former drug traffickers come from interviews with such people.

Information about Donnie Barrentine is from interviewing him at his home, the case file, and court testimony.

Details about the death of Greg Barrentine's children are from *Undisclosed*, interviews with relatives, and police records.

Donnie Barrentine acknowledged to me that he'd been suspected of different homicides, and he maintained his innocence in all. Bundy also told this to *Undisclosed*.

The email to the DA's office about Barrentine is in the case file.

Details of Bundy's interview with Kittrell are from the case file.

Information about what Perry's team learned about Jane Beaver is from court records and interviews.

The requests for Beaver's mental health hospitalization records are contained in the case file.

The note referencing "delusions" was first discovered and released by *Undisclosed*.

Perry told me he knew about Beaver's troubles and how he felt that she was a witness against him.

Information about the plea deal offered to Perry comes from court filings by Perry's attorneys.

The descriptions of John B. Johnson III comes from his interview in the BBC documentary *Life and Death Row*. "God gave me a gift and that gift is to be able to take a case and go to court and try it," Johnson told the filmmakers. "I consider myself to be directed by God to this line of work and to basically do my preaching in front of 12 jurors."

Johnson told me about his first case and how he witnessed the execution. He said he'd always been taken back to the moment of seeing the gruesome murder evidence every time he smelled death, such as from decaying roadkill. After the execution, Johnson said, the smell didn't bring back those unsettling flashbacks.

Perry told me about how he thought about the plea offer and why he turned it down.

14. SURPRISES

After many years spent covering hundreds of murder cases, I know how rare it is for a murder trial to take place after eighteen years. I know the dangers from my study in the Michigan Innocence Clinic. Most homicide cases that go to trial do so within a few years.

Johnson's and everyone else's statements and actions during the trial come from the trial transcript. Where I explain what someone was thinking or feeling, it comes from interviews with that person or other sources. For instance, I know the prosecution felt Beaver did well on the stand because there is a handwritten note, evidently passed between Johnson and his assistant, that says so.

Details about Beaver's traumas and losses come from newspaper accounts and interviews with people who knew her.

15. CAGED

Perry told me about his arrival at state prison and about the head shaving. I described the prisons based on my reporting on the Georgia Department of

Corrections, which has revealed numerous deficiencies in how the agency cares for prisoners, as well as persistent failure to keep prisoners safe.

Perry told me about his experiences and feelings in prison.

Perry and John, who asked me not to use his last name to avoid unfair judgment for his past mistakes, told me about their relationship and what each meant to the other. They told me about how they never talked about their convictions until deep into their friendships and how each reacted.

Daniel Perry told me about the meeting with Kennedy. He gave me a copy of the letter he wrote and told me that no one responded.

Brenda (Hahn) Perry told me about noticing Dennis Perry when they were young, and he would come by the house selling fish. She told me about the bar and the kiss on the cheek.

Brenda Perry and, later, Dennis Perry told me about their first phone call.

Details about Brenda Perry's life come from interviews with her, her husband, relatives, and friends.

Brenda told me about her drive to visit Dennis and described visitation, as well as where it took place and how it all felt.

Interlude: The allegations in this scene come from an incident report prepared by the officer for the Glynn County Police Department. The information about Sparre's past arrests and allegations against him comes from court records and incident reports from the Glynn County Police Department.

16. BEGINNINGS AND ENDINGS

The scenes on the boat and on Cumberland Island are based on interviews in the GBI case file from the resulting investigation into Jim Stein's allegations.

John Edwards, who led the investigation, told me about the sheriff's response. I also studied the GBI case file, which includes an audio-recorded interview in which Smith strongly denies any wrongdoing. Smith wasn't charged. District Attorney Jackie Johnson decided, according to a letter she sent to the GBI, that there were concerns about the statute of limitations for the allegations against Smith.

Tommy and Joe Gregory told me about their call about the son running for sheriff.

Tommy Gregory told me why he ran for sheriff and how he felt about Sheriff Smith. In a 2012 "ad" in *The Camden County Press*, a "newspaper" Smith supporters printed and used to promote Smith's attempt to reclaim the sheriff's office from Gregory, Smith claimed that Gregory used seized drug money to help fund his brother's college. Smith, whose agency had used seized drug money to help fund college for people he knew, said he fired Gregory when he found out.

Information about how Smith spent the money comes from bank records, GBI interviews, my own interviews, and exposés in *The Tribune & Georgian* and *The Florida Times-Union*.

The reward information is from the GBI case file.

The sheriff's conflict with the Camden County Board of Commissioners played out in the pages of local newspapers and in interviews conducted by the GBI. The allegation about voice stress analysis is from the GBI case file.

The debate was covered in *The Tribune & Georgian* news article contained in the GBI case file.

I got the results of the election from *The Florida Times-Union*.

Kennedy, Gregory, and Perry told me their reaction to Smith's defeat.

Perry told me how it helped to have officers on his side.

Dennis and Brenda told me about the wedding. Before Perry was free, Brenda showed me a photo album from the day, and she told me how much it meant, in spite of the circumstances.

Michelle, who asked me not to use her last name to help keep her husband's identity private, told me about riding with Brenda Perry to visit John. Michelle and John told me about falling in love, getting married, and finally getting to enjoy the depth of their love every day once John was paroled.

Dennis Perry and John told me about when John was moved and how they worried they'd never see each other again but still were happy because it was great news for John. John and Michelle told me about John's work at the governor's mansion.

Perry told me about getting stabbed and punished.

17. UNDISCLOSED

In describing Susan Simpson, her thinking and her investigation, I relied on many conversations about the case with her, records she sent me, the unedited full tape of her interviews with Bundy, and listening to *Undisclosed*.

Kennedy told me he was exceedingly impressed with Simpson's work and hopeful because of it.

Details of Beaver's death and her diagnosis come from her obituary and interviews with people who knew her, including her family and other people who were close to her.

Foster's statements to Simpson are repeated in a sworn affidavit that was an exhibit in the filing to overturn Perry's conviction that resulted from Simpson's *Undisclosed* investigation.

The reason Foster's missing report could've led to Perry's conviction being overturned is that it was considered exculpatory material, which must be turned over to the defense since the 1963 landmark US Supreme Court decision *Brady v. Maryland*.

Simpson's interview with Raborn was on *Undisclosed*.

Perry told me about listening to *Undisclosed* and how it felt.

I know that the Georgia Department of Corrections had in recent decades developed a culture where prisoners weren't allowed to give interviews except about programs officials wanted to brag about. The only people in Georgia prisons I have ever spoken with were on contraband cell phones or in person while I was observing a program that officials were proud of.

Simpson's interviews with Owens and Lavinia were on *Undisclosed*.

Simpson told me what Bundy yelled into the phone and that he apologized.

PART III: THE TIDE COMES BACK

In describing hurricane patterns, I relied on my decades living in the region and reporting on hurricanes and tropical storms there, which involved interviewing untold residents about why they didn't evacuate.

I know how the water can bring small sea creatures into people's homes from seeing the aftermath of an underestimated storm in person in Camden County and Glynn County and interviewing residents of both during the cleanup.

18. THROUGH THE GLASS DOOR

I've seen the Confederate monument many times and experienced what's described.

I lived through the segregated-in-practice school segregation and the integration in the 1990s.

I know when Bundy retired from his personnel file.

19. "IF I HAD CONFESSED TO THAT"

I read excerpts of David Sparre's letter admitting to the murder in the *Flor-*

ida Times-Union. I interviewed the prosecutor who sent him to death row. I read court records from his case and watched the video of a 2020 hearing over whether his sentence should be reduced to life without parole.

20. "I NEED YOUR HELP"

Ron Grosse, the Georgia Innocence Project investigator who tried to get a DNA sample from an item Sparre discarded, testified in the hearing of Perry's motion to overturn his conviction about that and about how he got the hair sample from Gladys Sparre.

Information about the DNA testing prior to Perry's trial is from the case file.

I have the DNA test results, and to put it in context, I interviewed Simon A. Cole, a forensic science expert from the University of California, Irvine, who also reviewed the results.

Jennifer Whitfield told me how Perry and Kennedy reacted and what they said upon learning of the results. Brenda Perry told me how she felt.

Kennedy told me how he still blamed himself.

The timeline of when Perry's attorneys told the DA's office about the DNA match is according to the attorneys' statements in court.

21. MORE BLOOD, MORE RECKONING

Details of Ahmaud Arbery's murder come from court records and the video. Multiple people told me Sparre worked on the bridge. I also consulted Mitchell S. Jackson's heartbreaking essay "Twelve Minutes and a Life," which was published June 18, 2020, in *Runner's World.*

Barnhill's perspective on the case is from the letter he wrote to the district attorney he was forwarding the case to after recusing himself.

Arbery's heritage is noted in numerous articles, including "Remembering Gullah/Geechee Souls: A Requiem for Ahmaud Arbery and Revisiting Wilmington 1898 Massacre," published August 14, 2020, on gullahgeecheenation.com. The community's history is also explained on the site as well as on the website of the National Park Service.

Information about Georgia's citizen's arrest law and how it was abused is widely documented, but the May 14, 2020, Associated Press article by Jeff Amy, "Georgia Gov. Kemp Signs Repeal of 1863 Citizen's Arrest Law," provides helpful context and history.

I watched the fallout of the Arbery murder video on social media and in *The*

Atlanta Journal-Constitution, where my colleagues' reporting questioned various officials' actions in the case. The paper covered protests, the rise of the A Better Glynn advocacy group, and the swift arrest of the killers once the GBI got involved.

I learned from the GBI and people who knew Sparre how he was spending his time, some of what he was thinking, and why he wanted to move out of the place he was sharing with his mom.

The information about people who told the GBI of Sparre's incriminating statements is from the audio recordings of the interviews, which I obtained from the courthouse.

I knew about the email the DA's office sent to Perry's team from Perry's lawyers.

Perry told me he was in the same room where he'd listened to *Undisclosed*.

Ekonomou's work for Trump was widely publicized.

I attended the hearing and, in describing it, relied on my notes and in large part a video of the hearing filmed by Ryon Horne, which is available on YouTube on *The Atlanta Journal-Constitution*'s channel.

Interlude: Brenda Perry told me about Sparre's son's visit to her house to apologize.

22. A DECISION AND A DEATH

I learned about Sparre's alibi for the time of his mother's death, and his denials that he had anything to do with it, from the GBI and other people who knew him.

The GBI told me that the autopsy was inconclusive and that it was doing further testing.

Everything in the bond hearing comes from what I witnessed outside with Perry's supporters and from the video filmed inside the courtroom by Ryon Horne and footage film outside by Tyson Horne.

Dennis and Brenda told me about his first days home, as did others who knew him, including longtime friend Clayton Tomlinson, who visited from Texas.

In telling about the search warrant execution on Sparre's property, I used my observations, photos, and videos from being there, as well as video and photos from Ryon and Tyson Horne.

A GBI source told me that, at least at first glance, the search didn't appear to uncover any new evidence of Sparre's involvement in the Swains' murders.

I heard about the Florida trip from a source who asked to remain anonymous. The GBI knew they were going.

A GBI official told me how they descended on the house and pressed Sparre and his brother and sister-in-law and how they responded to the pressure.

I've seen photos of Kenneth Metts and have his date of birth. The GBI told me the details included about him. I heard from a GBI official how agents weren't swayed by the idea of Metts doing the murders.

Interlude: From a distance, I witnessed the exhumation of Harold Swain's body, documenting it with photos, notes, and videos. I also used photos from Ryon and Tyson Horne.

23. ENDINGS

I described the hearing and its aftermath from my own observations—being there and documenting with written notes and audio and video recording, as well as footage filmed by T. J. Thompson for the Georgia Innocence Project.

I've covered Georgia's compensation mechanism and spoken with lawmakers who've tried to reform it. I also covered the bill to compensate Perry. Jeff Anderson, who lived in the same area of Brantley County as Greg Barrentine, told me that he often also saw Erik Sparre there in the 1980s.

Interlude: This scene is from footage filmed by Ryon Horne for *The Imperfect Alibi*, a documentary made by *The Atlanta Journal-Constitution* photo staff to accompany my reporting on the church murders. Jackie Johnson, who maintained her innocence, was ultimately not convicted in the case against her related to her handling of the Ahmaud Arbery murder.

EPILOGUE

Information on Sparre's life comes from interviews with officials and people who know him. Information on his arrest is from police sources as well as public records. I spoke with Charlie Swain and saw his sister Pearl Cole's post praising the arrest and the power of prayer on the day after Sparre was booked.

Kalem Head told me about his feelings around his mother's murder and who might've been responsible. He told me that his mother's accused killer, Theron Hendrix, died in what officials called a suicide in state prison in early 2024. The prosecutor I spoke with about the murder of Head's mom was Nigel Lush.

Dennis Perry told me the story about telling Kennedy the news of Sparre's arrest, and Jennifer Whitfield, who called Perry while he was at Kennedy's house, corroborated it.

INDEX

Page numbers after 214 refer to notes.